Knitted Mitts & Mittens

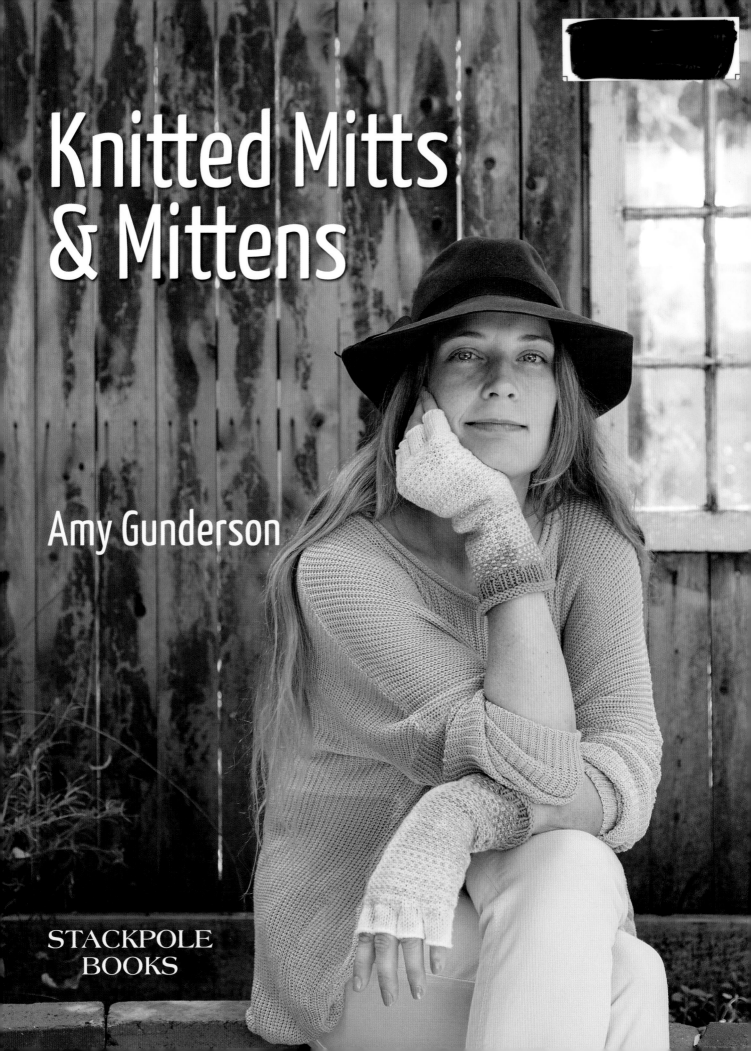

Knitted Mitts & Mittens

Amy Gunderson

STACKPOLE
BOOKS

To my mom, who has patiently supported me,
from tomboy to rebellious teen and through
unexpected adulthood paths, and who always
made me believe I was special and loved.

Published by
STACKPOLE BOOKS
5067 Ritter Road
Mechanicsburg, PA 17055
www.stackpolebooks.com

Printed in U.S.A.
10 9 8 7 6 5 4 3 2 1
First edition

Photos of finished projects by Burcu Avsar
Step-by-step photos by Amy Gunderson
Front cover photo by Burcu Avsar
Cover design by Wendy A. Reynolds

Library of Congress Cataloging-in-Publication Data

Gunderson, Amy.
    Knitted mitts & mittens / Amy Gunderson.
        pages cm
    ISBN 978-0-8117-1299-6
    1. Knitting—Patterns. 2. Gloves. I. Title. II. Title: Knitted mitts
and mittens.
TT825.G7847   2014
746.43'2—dc23
                                                2013041568

Acknowledgments

A big hug and kiss to my ever-supportive husband, Kirk. He hasn't once complained about all the fabric, yarn, and other assorted crafty stuff I've accumulated over the decade we've been together. Although I try not to talk about knitting *all* the time, when I do, he can hold up his end of the conversation. For that, I am very grateful.

I would like to thank Rae Blackledge, my friend, co-worker, and technical editor of these patterns. Rae was also the willing and knowledgeable hand model in all the tutorial photos. Thanks, Rae, for allowing me to be able to say, "Okay, now do some stranded knitting!" and give you almost no other direction than just that.

I'd like to give a shout out to Lisa Shroyer, former editor of *Knitscene,* now editor of *Interweave Knits* and *Knit.Wear.* When I submitted two ideas to Lisa for *Knitscene* two and a half years ago (having never published a knitting pattern before), she accepted them both. I was a random nobody and she took a chance on me. Thanks for the faith, Lisa!

Michael del Vecchio and Hal Ozbelli of Premier Yarns also took a chance on me when they hired me in April 2012 as design coordinator. I had only a few years of knitting and a handful of published patterns under my belt, but for some crazy reason they thought I could handle doing the designing thing professionally. Thank you so much for believing in me and giving me a job!

The strikingly creative photos in this book are the work of talented photographer Burcu Avsar. She brought each and every one of these projects to life most delightfully. Lovely job, Burcu!

Lastly, I'd like to heap my gratitude upon Pam Hoenig, my editor at Stackpole Books. Throughout the journey of this book over the past nine months, Pam has been extremely helpful, insightful, and all-around great to work with. I was able to exercise ultimate creative control over the projects in the book, from yarn choice and color to design, and got nothing but support from Pam along the way. The ability to be free in this decision making allowed me to unleash many ideas that easily could have been stifled in other circumstances. Pam, thank you for stepping in when you needed to, and otherwise allowing me to do what I do.

Contents

Introduction

I love to knit sweaters, with their seemingly endless design possibilities: pullover or cardigan? Raglan, drop-shoulder, or set-in sleeves? Colorwork or texture? V-neck, roll neck, boat neck, or crew neck? And there are so many ways to add your own personal bit of flair. After all, we do this because we want to make a unique knitted "thing" that reflects who we are, right?

When I was approached to do this book, my first thought was "Gloves? Gosh, how in the world can I come up with 25 distinctive designs for hands?" Mitts seemed inconsequential, with little room for fun and exploration. But the more I started sketching out designs and playing around with different ideas, the more smitten I was with the concept. Instead of sleeve options, I was brainstorming interesting ways to make a thumb gusset. Instead of deciding between a pullover and a cardigan, I was thinking, flat-knit gloves or worked in the round? I've come to realize that though the canvas may be smaller with gloves, there are still lots of opportunities for customization and creativity. My own personal style is an eclectic mix of feminine, edgy, conservative, and bohemian; in the following pages, you will find evidence of this. I truly hope you enjoy making these projects as much as I did designing them.

This book was designed with every knitter in mind. Fingerless gloves and mittens are the perfect project for quick gratification, to learn a new technique, and to knit on the go. Been itching to give stranded knitting a try? Check out Beetle Mitts (page 77) or Gradient Mittens (page 23). Ready for more advanced colorwork? Energy Mitts on page 50 use shaped intarsia to achieve smooth, flowing lines. (Be sure to visit the guide in the back of the book for photo tutorials on stitches and special techniques used in this book.) Need a quick gift for a special man or woman in your life? Big and Little Bamboo Mitts incorporate simple knit-purl texture to create the perfect unisex fingerless mitt. Young or old, beginner or advanced, looking for an adventure or just a relaxing knit, *Knitted Mitts & Mittens* has a project for you!

Coventry

R ustic, textured, classic: Coventry Mitts have it
all. They begin with a garter stitch–based rib at
the cuff. The stockinette-stitch hand has a center panel worked in a slip-stitch pattern resembling
diamond quilting.

NEEDLES AND OTHER MATERIALS
• US 5 (3.75 mm) set of 5 double-pointed needles (dpns)
• Tapestry needle
• Stitch markers
• Waste yarn
• Two $7/8$"/2 cm shank buttons

GAUGE
20 sts x 26 rows in rev St st = 4"/10 cm square
Be sure to check your gauge!

NOTES
• When slipping stitches on Rows 1 and 5 of Quilting
patt, take care not to pull the yarn tightly across your
work.
• You will use a knitted cast-on for the I-Cord Bind-Off
(see page 101 for a tutorial).

FINISHED MEASUREMENTS
Hand circumference: $7\frac{1}{4}$ (8, $8\frac{3}{4}$)"/ 18.5 (20.5, 22) cm
Length: $7\frac{1}{4}$ ($7\frac{3}{4}$, $8\frac{1}{2}$)"/ 18.5 (19.5, 21.5) cm

YARN
Deborah Norville Wool Naturals by Premier Yarns,
medium worsted weight #4 yarn (100% wool; 205 yd/
3.5 oz, 187 m/100 g per skein)
• 1 skein #425-05 Chocolate

STITCH GUIDE

Quilting Pattern (worked over 15 sts)

Row 1: K2, * sl 5 pwise wyif, k1; rep from * once more, k1.

Even-numbered Rows 2-6: Knit.

Row 3: K4; insert RH needle under loose strand and knit next st, pulling st under strand (quilting st made); k5, quilting st, k4.

Row 5: K1, sl 3 pwise wyif, k1, sl 5 pwise wyif, k1, sl 3 pwise wyif, k1.

Row 7: K1, * quilting st, k5; rep from * once more, quilting st, k1.

Row 8: Knit.

Rep Rows 1-8 for patt.

Garter Rib (multiple of 3 sts)

Rnds 1–3: * K2, p1; rep from * to end.

Rnd 4: Purl.

Rep Rnds 1-4 for patt.

Right Mitt

Cuff

With A, CO 30 (33, 36) sts. Divide evenly between 4 dpns and join to work in the rnd.

Work Rnds 1-4 of Garter Rib 4 times.

Hand

Inc rnd: K0 (2, 3), * k5, m1L; rep from * 5 (6, 7) more times, knit to end—36 (40, 44) sts.

Purl 1 rnd.

Establish Pattern

Setup rnd: P1 (2, 3) pm, k15, pm, purl to end.

Rnd 1: Purl to m, work Row 1 of Quilting patt to m, purl to end.

Rnd 2: Purl to m, work Row 2 of Quilting patt to m, purl to end.

Rnds 3 & 4: Work even in patt as set.

Thumb Gusset

Rnd 1: Purl to m, work Row 5 of Quilting patt to m, p4 (5, 6), pm for Thumb, m1P, pm, purl to end—1 st inc'd.

Rnd 2: Purl to m, work Row 6 of Quilting patt to Thumb m, purl to end.

Rnd 3: Purl to m, work Row 7 of patt to Thumb m, m1P, purl to 1 st bef m, m1P, purl to end—2 sts inc'd.

Rnd 4: Purl to m, work Row 8 of patt to Thumb m, purl to m, purl to end.

Rnd 5: Purl to m, work Row 1 of patt to Thumb m, m1P, purl to 1 st bef m, m1P, purl to end—2 sts inc'd.

Rnd 6: Purl to m, work Row 2 of patt to Thumb m, purl to m, purl to end.

Rnd 7: Purl to m, work Row 3 of patt to Thumb m, m1P, purl to 1 st bef m, m1P, purl to end—2 sts inc'd.

Rnd 8: Purl to m, work Row 4 of patt to Thumb m, purl to m, purl to end.

Rnd 9: Purl to m, work Row 5 of patt to Thumb m, m1P, purl to 1 st bef m, m1P, purl to end—2 sts inc'd.

Rnd 10: Purl to m, work Row 6 of patt to Thumb m, purl to m, purl to end.

Rnd 11: Purl to m, work Row 7 of patt to Thumb m, m1P, purl to 1 st bef m, m1P, purl to end—2 sts inc'd.

Rnd 12: Purl to m, work Row 8 of patt to Thumb m, purl to m, purl to end.

Rnd 13: Purl to m, work Row 1 of patt to Thumb m, m1P, purl to 1 st bef m, m1P, purl to end—2 sts inc'd.

Rnd 14: Purl to m, work Row 2 of patt to Thumb m, purl to m, purl to end.

Rnd 15: Purl to m, work Row 3 of patt to Thumb m, m1P, purl to 1 st bef m, m1P, purl to end—2 sts inc'd.

Rnd 16: Purl to m, work Row 4 of patt to Thumb m, purl to m, purl to end—15 Thumb sts.

Medium and Large Sizes Only

Rnd 17: Purl to m, work Row 5 of patt to Thumb m, m1P, purl to 1 st bef m, m1P, purl to end—2 sts inc'd.

Rnd 18: Purl to m, work Row 6 of patt to Thumb m, purl to m, purl to end—17 Thumb sts.

Large Size Only

Rnd 19: Purl to m, work Row 7 of patt to Thumb m, m1P, purl to 1 st bef m, m1P, purl to end—2 sts inc'd.

Rnd 20: Purl to m, work Row 8 of patt to Thumb m, purl to m, purl to end—19 Thumb sts.

Upper Hand

All Sizes

Next rnd: Work in patt to Thumb m, remove m, slip 15 (17, 19) Thumb sts onto waste yarn, remove m, purl to end—36 (40, 44) sts rem.

Work in patt for 10 (12, 14) more rnds, ending with Row 7 (3, 7) of Quilting patt.

[Knit 1 rnd. Purl 1 rnd] 3 times.

I-Cord Bind-off

CO 3 sts to LH needle. * K2, k2tog tbl (1 st bound off), sl these 3 sts back to LH needle; rep from * until 3 sts rem. BO rem 3 I-Cord sts.

Thumb

Place held Thumb sts evenly on 3 dpns. Beg at center of Thumb gap, pick up and purl 2 sts, p15 (17, 19), pick up and purl 1—18 (20, 22) sts.

Dec rnd: P1, p2tog, purl to last 2 sts, p2tog—16 (18, 20) sts rem.

Purl 3 rnds.

Knit 1 rnd. BO all sts loosely pwise.

Left Mitt

Cuff

Work as for Right Mitt.

Hand

Inc rnd: K0 (2, 3), * k5, m1; rep from * 5 (6, 7) more times, knit to end—36 (40, 44) sts.

Purl 1 rnd.

Establish Pattern

Setup rnd: P2 (3, 4) pm, k15, pm, purl to end.

Rnd 1: Purl to m, work Row 1 of Quilting patt to m, purl to end.

Rnd 2: Purl to m, work Row 2 of patt to m, purl to end.

Rnds 3 & 4: Work even in patt as set.

Thumb Gusset

Rnd 1: Work in patt to last 2 sts, pm, m1p, pm, p2—1 st inc'd.

Comp remainder of Left Mitt as for Right Mitt.

Finishing

I-Cord Button Band

CO 3 sts to one dpn. * Slide sts to other end of needle, place in left hand, k3; rep from * until I-Cord meas 6" (15 cm). BO all sts. Bring ends of I-Cord tog. Sew ends to Mitt at inner wrist just above last row of Cuff, Sew button to outer wrist at top of Cuff. Loop Button Band around button.

Weave in loose ends.

Kaleidoscope

Each of these colorful mitts is comprised of 12 hexagons worked from the outside in. The pattern for the hexagons is short and easy to memorize, making this a great travel project. Use a self-striping yarn such as Serenity Garden (shown) for a kaleidoscopic effect, or try different colored solids for more of a color-pop look. You could also consider working the first few rounds of each hexagon in one color, and the inner rounds in another color for a completely different feel. The possibilities are endless!

FINISHED MEASUREMENTS
Hand circumference: 7"/18 cm
Length: 6½"/16.5 cm

YARN
Deborah Norville Collection Serenity Garden by Premier Yarns, fine weight #2 yarn (100% microfiber; 185 yd/3 oz, 169 m/85 g per skein)
• 1 skein #800-08 Sea

NEEDLES AND OTHER MATERIALS
• US 3 (3.25 mm) set of 5 double-pointed needles (dpns)
• Tapestry needle
• Stitch markers

GAUGE

24 sts x 32 rows in St st = 4"/10 cm square

1 Hexagon = 2¼"/5.5 cm measured on the diagonal,
   2"/5 cm measured from flat edge to flat edge

Be sure to check your gauge!

NOTES

• See page 113 for a tutorial on how to work short rows.
• When casting on for the hexagons, use the backward-loop cast-on method (see page 103 for a tutorial).

STITCH GUIDE

Hexagon

Rnd 1: Knit.

Rnd 2: * K2tog, k2, ssk; rep from * to end—24 sts rem.

Rnds 3 & 4: Knit.

Rnd 5: * K2tog, ssk; rep from * to end—12 sts rem.

Rnd 6: * K2tog, ssk; rep from * to end—6 sts rem. Break yarn, thread through tapestry needle. Pass through rem live sts, pull taut, fasten off.

Right Mitt

Middle Tier

Hexagon 1: CO 36 sts. Divide evenly between 3 dpns and join to work in the rnd. Work Rnds 1-6 of Hexagon.

Hexagon 2: CO 30 sts, pick up and knit 6 sts from one side of Hexagon 1—36 sts. Divide evenly between 3 dpns and join to work in the rnd. Work Rnds 1-6 of Hexagon.

Hexagon 3 (Thumb): CO 30 sts, pick up and knit 6 sts from one side of Hexagon 2—36 sts. Divide evenly between 3 dpns and join to work in the rnd. Work Rnds 1-3 of Hexagon. BO rem 24 sts pwise.

Hexagon 4: CO 12 sts, pick up and knit 6 sts from one side of Hexagon 3, CO 12, pick up and knit 6 sts from side of Hexagon 1—36 sts. Divide evenly between 3 dpns and join to work in the rnd. Work Rnds 1-6 of Hexagon.

Upper Tier

Hexagon 5: CO 24 sts, pick up and knit 6 sts from Hexagon 1, pick up and knit 6 sts from Hexagon 2—36 sts. Divide evenly between 3 dpns and join to work in the rnd. Work Rnds 1–6 of Hexagon.

Hexagon 6: CO 18 sts, pick up and knit 6 sts from Hexagons 5, 2, & 3—36 sts. Comp Hexagon as described above.

Hexagon 7: CO 18 sts, pick up and knit 6 sts from Hexagons 6, 3, & 4—36 sts. Comp Hexagon as described above.

Hexagon 8: CO 12 sts, pick up and knit 6 sts from Hexagons 7, 4, & 1, CO 6, pick up and knit 6 sts from Hexagon 5—36 sts. Comp Hexagon as described above.

Lower Tier

Comp as for Upper Tier.

Left Mitt

Comp as for Right Mitt.

Hand Construction

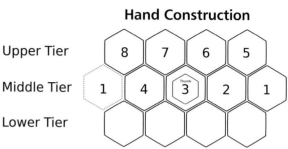

Upper Tier

Middle Tier

Lower Tier

Finishing

Upper Edging

Beg at valley bet 2 hexagons on Upper Tier, * pick up and knit 6 sts to peak of hexagon, pick up and knit 6 sts to valley; rep from * 3 more times—48 sts. Divide evenly between 4 dpns, join to work in the rnd.

Rnd 1: Purl.

Rnd 2: * K2tog, k3, [kfb] twice, k3, ssk; rep from * to end. BO all sts pwise.

Lower Edging

Beg at peak of any hexagon, * pick up and knit 6 sts to valley, pick up and knit 6 sts to peak; rep from * 3 more times—48 sts. Divide evenly between 4 dpns, join to work in the rnd.

Shape Lower Edging with Short Rows

Row 1: K7, w&t.

Row 2 (WS): P2, w&t.

Row 3: K2, knit next st tog with wrap, k1, w&t.

Row 4: P4, ssp next st tog with wrap, p1, w& t.

Row 5: K6, knit next st tog with wrap, k2.

Rep Rows 1–5 three more times.

Next rnd: Purl, leaving rem wraps unworked.

Next rnd: Knit.

Dec rnd: * K2, p2tog; rep from * to end—32 sts rem.

Next rnd: * K2, p1; rep from * to end. Rep this rnd 6 more times. BO all sts in patt.

Weave in ends.

> **TIP** ✳ Consider using both the center strand and the outer strand from your ball of yarn. That way, you can have different colors to choose from at all times, and can pick just the right color for your next hexagon.

Independence

Wondering what to wear to your next Fourth of July barbecue? Problem solved. Not a fan of barbecues? For a more versatile look, try choosing tonal colors or omitting the striping sequence and opting for a solid-color hand. The mitts are knit first; the star appliqué is knit separately and sewn on.

FINISHED MEASUREMENTS
Hand circumference: 7 (8, 9)"/18 (20.5, 23) cm
Length: 5 (6, 6¾)"/12.5 (15, 17) cm

YARN
Premier Yarns Cotton Fair, fine #2 yarn (52% cotton, 48% acrylic; 317 yd/3.5 oz, 290 m/100g per skein)
• 1 skein #3202 Blue Ice (MC)
• 1 skein #2702 Cream (CC1)
• 1 skein #2708 Red (CC2)

NEEDLES AND OTHER MATERIALS
• US 3 (3.25 mm) set of 5 double-pointed needles (dpns)
• Tapestry needle
• Stitch markers
• Waste yarn
• US D-3 (3.25 mm) crochet hook, sewing needle and thread

GAUGE
24 sts x 30 rows in St st = 4"/10 cm square
Be sure to check your gauge!

NOTES
• When casting on stitches for Thumb Gusset, use backward-loop method (see page 103 for a tutorial).

STITCH GUIDE
Wrap 3 Stitches (W-3)
Sl next 3 sts pwise wyib, take yarn to front of work, sl same 3 sts back to LH needle, take yarn to back of work, sl same 3 sts back to RH needle (yarn has been wrapped once around 3 stitches). When wrapping sts, be sure not to pull yarn too tightly; keep yarn at a tension even to the knitting itself.

Stripe Sequence
Rnds 1 & 2: With CC1, knit.
Rnds 3 & 4: With MC, knit.
Rep Rnds 1-4 for patt.

Right Mitt
Cuff
With MC, CO 42 (48, 54) sts. Divide evenly between 4 dpns and join to work in the rnd.
Rnd 1: Purl.
Rnd 2: Knit.
Rnds 3 & 4: Rep Rnds 1 & 2.
Rnd 5: With CC2, * W-3; rep from * to end.
Rnds 6 & 7: Rep Rnds 1 & 2.
Rnds 8–10: Rep Rnds 5–7.

Hand
Beg with Rnd 1 of Stripe Sequence, work 4 rnds in Stripe Sequence patt.
Note: Cont to work in Stripe Sequence throughout remainder of Hand.

Thumb Gusset

Rnd 1: Knit to last 9 (10, 12) sts, pm, m1L, pm, knit to end—1 st inc'd.

Rnd 2: Knit.

Rnd 3: Knit to m, CO 1 st, knit to m, CO 1 st, knit to end—2 sts inc'd.

Rnd 4: Knit.

Rep last 2 rnds 8 (9, 10) more times—19 (21, 23) Thumb sts.

Next rnd: Knit to m, remove m, place Thumb sts on waste yarn, remove m, knit to end—42 (48, 54) sts rem.

Cont in Stripe Sequence, work 5 (7, 9) more rnds. Break CC1.

Upper Edging

Rnd 1: Knit

Rnd 2: Purl.

Rnd 3: Knit.

Rnd 4: With CC2, * W-3; rep from * to end.

Rnds 5–7: Rep Rnds 2–4.

Rnds 8 & 9: Rep Rnds 2 & 3.

BO all sts pwise.

Thumb

Place held Thumb sts evenly onto 3 dpns. Beg at center of Thumb gap, with MC, pick up and knit 2 sts, k19 (21, 23), pick up and knit 1 st—22 (24, 26) sts.

Dec rnd: P1, p2tog, purl to last 3 sts, p2tog, p1—20 (22, 24) sts rem.

BO all sts loosely pwise.

Left Mitt

Work as for Right Mitt to Thumb Gusset.

Thumb Gusset

Rnd 1: K9 (10, 12), pm, kfb, pm, work in patt to end—1 st inc'd.

Comp as for Right Mitt.

Finishing

Star Appliqué (make 2)

With MC, CO 5 sts. Divide evenly between 3 dpns and join to work in the rnd. PM for beg of rnd.

Star Body

Rnd 1: Knit.

Rnd 2: * Kfb; rep from * to end—10 sts.

Rnd 3: * K1, kfb; rep from * to end—15 sts.

Rnd 4: * K2, kfb; rep from * to end—20 sts.

Rnd 5: * K3, kfb; rep from * to end—25 sts.

Rnd 6: * K4, kfb; rep from * to end—30 sts.

Rnd 7: * K5, kfb; rep from * to end—35 sts.

Rnd 8: K4.

Note: Rnd 8 is a partial round that serves to get you to the right place to begin the first point.

Star Point

Row 1 (RS): K2, sl2, k1, p2sso, k2, turn—5 sts rem.

Row 2 (WS): Purl.

Row 3: K1, sl2, k1, p2sso, k1—3 sts rem.

Row 4: Purl.

Row 5: Sl2, k1, p2sso—1 st rem. Break yarn, fasten off last st.

Attach yarn to st left of base of Star Point just worked. Work Rows 1–5 of Star Point. Rep for each of the 3 rem Star Points.

Crochet Edging

Attach CC2 to Star between any 2 Points.

Rnd 1: With crochet hook, * work 5 sl st up side of Point, [sl st, ch 1, sl st] in top of point, work 5 sl st down other side of Point; rep from * for rem 4 Points, join with sl st to beg sl st. Fasten off.

Position Star Appliqué on back of hand and pin in place. Sew onto Mitt with sewing needle and thread. Rep with other Star Appliqué.

Weave in loose ends.

Oasis
Mitts

The name of these darling mitts, Oasis, may seem ironic. Typically, an oasis is a refuge, a relief, a safe place, right? The "oasis" on the back of these mitts is swirling with decreases and increases, some of which you may have never done before. The Oasis chart might seem intimidating and the furthest thing from a haven, but I invite you to grab a refreshing beverage, sit down, and give it a whirl. Using a row counter to keep track of which row you're on can make it easier, as can using stitch markers to define the area for the chart as instructed in the pattern.

FINISHED MEASUREMENTS
Hand circumference: 7 (7¾)"/18 (19.5) cm
Length: 7 (7½)"/18 (19) cm

YARN
Premier Yarns Afternoon Cotton, DK weight #3 yarn (100% Egyptian Giza mercerized cotton; 136 yd/1.75 oz, 124 m/50g per skein)
• 1 skein #22-03 Bright Blue

NEEDLES AND OTHER MATERIALS
• US 3 (3.25 mm) 2 sets of 5 double-pointed needles (dpns)
• Tapestry needle
• Stitch markers
• Waste yarn

GAUGE
23 sts x 32 rows in St st = 4"/10 cm square
Be sure to check your gauge!

NOTES
• This mitt is worked from the top to the cuff. The Scalloped Edging is knit sideways around the bottom of the mitt, at the same time as the mitt stitches are bound off.
• See page 103 for a tutorial on crochet provisional cast-on. The Cuff uses a knitted cast-on (page 101).

STITCH GUIDE

Central Double Increase (CDI)
[K1 tbl, k1] into next st, insert LH needle behind vertical strand running down from between 2 sts just made, k1 tbl into this strand—2 sts inc'd.

Knit One Below
Knit into the back of the st below the next st on LH needle, knit next st—1 st inc'd.

Purl One Below
Purl into the back of the st below the next st on LH needle, purl next st—1 st inc'd.

Five into One
Sl 3 wyib, [pass 2nd st on RH needle over 1st (center) st, sl center st back to LH needle, and pass 2nd st on LH needle over it], sl center st back to RH needle, rep between [ ], knit center st—4 sts dec'd.

Cluster 3 (Cl-3)
Sl 3 wyib, bring yarn to front, sl the same 3 sts back to LH needle, take yarn to back, k3.

Key

☐	knit on RS, purl on WS
O	yo
╱	k2tog
╲	ssk
⋀	s1-k2tog-psso
●	purl on RS
V	CDI
V	knit 1 below
v̇	purl 1 below
⅍	5 into 1
╱ᵇ	k2tog tbl
b	knit 1 tbl
⊟	sl 1 wyif
╱.	p2tog
⟋	k3tog
⟍	sssk
⊢⊣	Cl-3
☐	patt rep
▨	no stitch

Oasis Pattern

13 st panel

Scalloped Edging

Left Mitt

CO 40 (44) sts using a crochet provisional CO. Divide sts evenly between 4 dpns and join to work in the rnd.

Knit 5 rnds. Purl 1 rnd. Knit 6 rnds.

Carefully place CO sts onto 4 spare dpns.

Next rnd: * Knit 1 st from main needles tog with 1 st from spare needles; rep from * to end—40 (44) sts.

Hand

Knit 3 (5) rnds.

Next rnd: K 3 (4), pm, work Row 1 of Oasis chart over 13 sts, pm, knit to end.

Next rnd: Knit to m, work next row of chart to m, knit to end.

Cont in patt through Row 12 of Oasis patt.

Set aside.

Thumb

CO 18 (20) sts. Divide sts evenly between 4 dpns and join to work in the rnd. Knit 5 (7) rnds. Break yarn, set aside.

Note: To reduce the number of times you have to break off and rejoin yarn, pull yarn from the other end of the skein for the thumb.

Thumb Gusset

Take up needles for Hand again.

Rnd 1: Knit to m, work Row 13 of Oasis patt to m, k5 (7), pm, sl 1, sl this st back to LH Thumb needle, ssk, knit to last Thumb st, sl 1, sl this st back to LH needle, k2tog, pm, knit to end—2 sts dec'd, 56 (62) sts rem.

Rnd 2: Knit to m, work Row 14 of Oasis patt to m, knit to end.

Rnd 3: Knit to m, work Row 15 of Oasis patt to m, k5 (7), sl 1, sl this st back to LH Thumb needle, ssk, knit to last Thumb st, sl 1, sl this st back to LH needle, k2tog, pm, knit to end—2 sts dec'd, 54 (60) sts rem.

Rnd 4: Knit to m, work Row 16 of Oasis patt to m, knit to end.

Rnd 5: [Knit to m, remove m] twice, knit to m, ssk, knit to 2 sts bef m, k2tog, knit to end—52 (58) sts rem.

Rnd 6: Knit.

Rnd 7: Knit to m, ssk, knit to 2 sts bef m, k2tog, knit to end—50 (56) sts rem.

Rnd 8: Knit.

Rep last 2 rnds 5 (6) more times—40 (44) sts rem.

Cuff

Next rnd: * K6 (9), k2tog; rep from * to end—35 (40) sts rem. Using knitted CO, CO 4 sts to LH needle. Work Rows 1-10 of Scalloped Edging chart 7 (8) times—4 Edging sts rem. BO rem sts kwise.

Right Mitt

Work as for Left Mitt through Hand.

Thumb Gusset

Rnd 1: Knit to m, work Row 13 of Oasis patt to m, knit to last 3 (4) sts, pm, sl 1, sl this st back to LH Thumb needle, ssk, knit to last Thumb st, sl 1, sl this st back to LH needle, k2tog, pm, knit to end—2 sts dec'd, 56 (62) sts rem.

Comp as for Left Mitt.

Finishing

Sew ends of Edging tog. Weave in loose ends. Wet block to tame Edging curl.

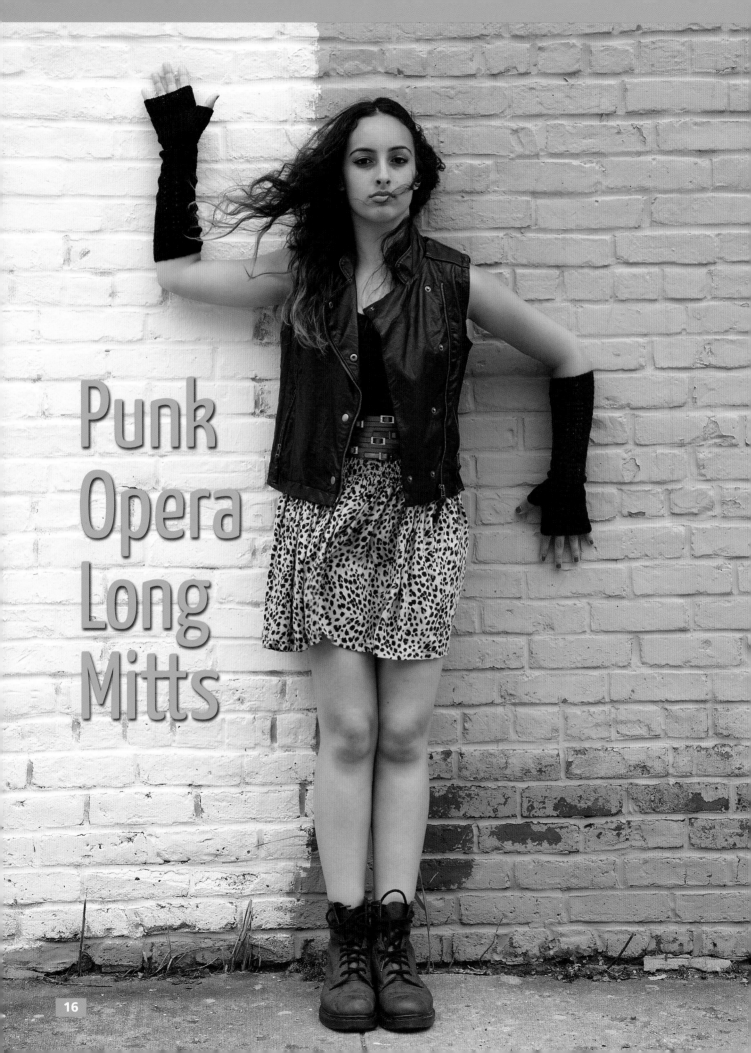

Punk
Opera
Long
Mitts

W orked in stretchy lace and ribbing, Punk Opera Mitts are designed to hug your arm and hand. Knit them as shown in black for a dramatic look and wear them with your best tough-chick boots. Or for a completely different feel, consider using white, cream, or pink. Wear them with your cutest floral dress, a cropped cardigan, and flats for maximum girly cuteness.

FINISHED MEASUREMENTS
Forearm circumference: 9"/ 23 cm unstretched; 12"/30.5 cm stretched
Hand circumference: 5½"/14 cm unstretched; 8½"/21.5 cm stretched
Length: 13½"/34.5 cm
Note: These mitts are very stretchy! One size fits most.

YARN
Deborah Norville Collection Serenity Sock Solids by Premier Yarns, superfine weight #1 yarn (50% superwash merino, 25% rayon from bamboo, 25% nylon; 230 yd/1.75 oz, 210 m/50 g per skein)
• 2 skeins #150-12 Black

NEEDLES AND OTHER MATERIALS
• US 1 (2.25 mm) set of 5 double-pointed needles (dpn)
• 2 spare US 1 (2.25 mm) or smaller circular needles or dpns
• Tapestry needle
• Stitch markers
• Waste yarn

GAUGE
30 sts x 44 rows in St st = 4"/10 cm square
Be sure to check your gauge!

STITCH GUIDE
Twisted Rib (even number of sts)
Rnd 1: * K1 tbl, p1; rep from * to end.
Rep Rnd 1 for patt.

Twisted Rib (odd number of sts)
Rnd 1: * K1 tbl, p1; rep from * to last st, k1 tbl.
Rep Rnd 1 for patt.

Right Hand

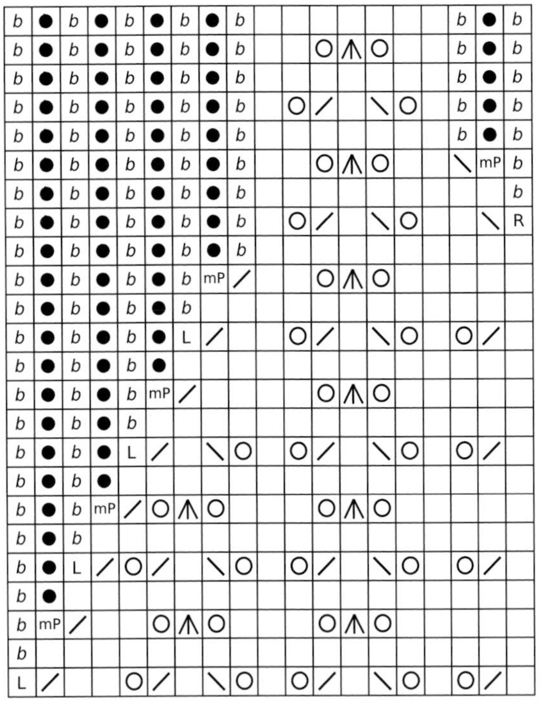
24, 28, 32, 36
23, 37, 31, 35
22, 26, 30, 34
21, 25, 29, 33
20
19
18
17
16
15
14
13
12
11
10
9
8
7
6
5
4
3
2
1

Arm

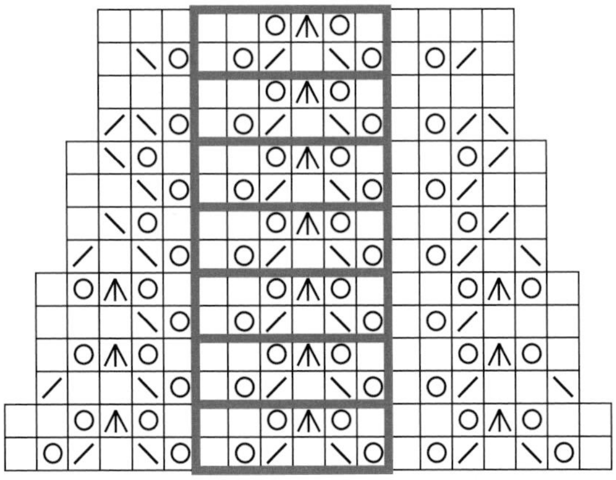
63, 67, 71, 75
61, 65, 69, 73
59
57
43, 47, 51, 55
41, 45, 49, 53
39
37
23, 27, 31, 35
21, 25, 29, 33
19
17
3, 7, 11, 15
1, 5, 9, 13,

Note: Knit all even numbered rnds 2-76

Left Hand

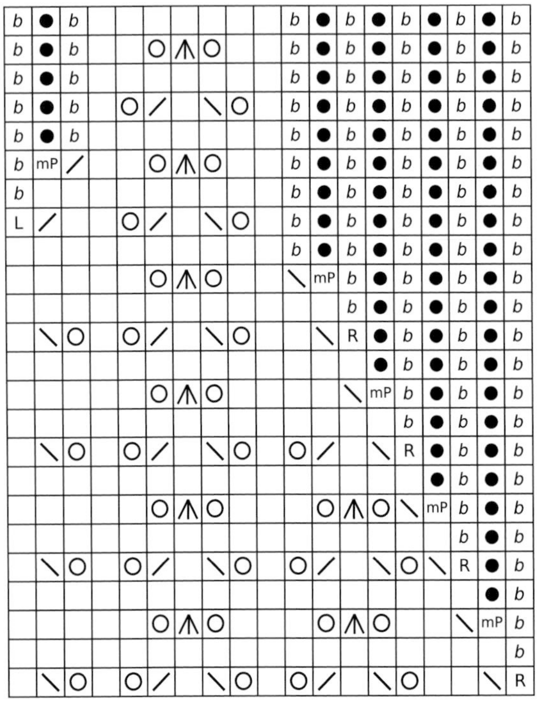
24, 28, 32, 36
23, 37, 31, 35
22, 26, 30, 34
21, 25, 29, 33
20
19
18
17
16
15
14
13
12
11
10
9
8
7
6
5
4
3
2
1

Key

- □ knit
- ○ yo
- ⁄ k2tog
- ⍀ ssk
- ⋀ s2-k1-psso
- ● purl
- L make 1 left
- R make 1 right
- mP make 1 purl
- *b* k1 tbl
- ▢ patt rep

Right Mitt

CO 60 sts. Divide evenly between 4 dpns and join to work in the rnd.

Cuff

Work 7 rnds in Twisted Rib.

Arm

Setup rnd: * K25, pm, [p1, k1] twice, p1, pm; rep from * once more.

Rnd 1: * Work Rnd 1 of Arm chart to m, work in Twisted Rib to m; rep from * once more.

Cont in patt, maint 5 sts on each side in Twisted Rib, through Row 76 of Arm chart—48 sts rem.

Hand

Rnd 1: Work Row 1 of Right Hand chart to m, [p1, k1] twice, pm for Thumb, p1, pm, work in Twisted Rib to end.

Rnd 2: Work Row 2 of Right Hand chart to m, work in Twisted Rib to end.

Thumb Gusset

Inc rnd: Work in patt to Thumb m, m1L, p1, m1R, work in patt to end—2 sts inc'd.

Next rnd: Work in patt to Thumb m, k1 tbl, p1, k1 tbl, work in Twisted Rib to end.

Inc rnd: Work in patt to Thumb m, m1p, work in Twisted Rib to m, m1p, work in patt to end—2 sts inc'd, 5 Thumb sts.

Next rnd: Work in patt.

Repeat last 4 rnds 4 more times—21 Thumb sts.

Next rnd: Work in patt to thumb m, remove m, place Thumb sts on waste yarn, CO 1 st using backward lp method, work in Twisted Rib to end—48 sts rem.

Work in patt through Row 36 of Right Hand chart. Work 7 rnds even in Twisted Rib.

Bind Off

Holding 2 circular needles or dpns parallel, slip first (knit) st to front needle, second (purl) st to back needle, third st to front needle, and so on, until all knit sts are on front needle and all purl sts are on back needle. BO all sts using Kitchener stitch.

Thumb

Place 21 held Thumb sts evenly onto 3 dpns. Beg at center of Thumb gap, pick up and knit 2 sts, work in Twisted Rib over 21 sts, pick up and knit 1—24 sts.

Dec rnd: K2tog, work in Twisted Rib to last 3 sts, ssk, p1—22 sts rem. Work 2 rnds even in Twisted Rib. BO all sts loosely kwise.

Left Mitt

CO 60 sts. Divide sts evenly between 4 dpns and join to work in the rnd.

Work as for Right Mitt to Hand section.

Hand

Rnd 1: Work Row 1 of Left Hand chart to m, work in Twisted Rib to last 5 sts, pm for Thumb, p1, pm, work in Twisted Rib to end.

Rnd 2: Work Row 2 of Left Hand chart to m, work in Twisted Rib to end.

Comp remainder of Left Mitt as for Right Mitt.

Finishing

Weave in loose ends. Wet block to even out lace patt.

Moroccan Tile Wristers

Do you ever finish getting dressed for the day and think, "Hmm, this outfit just needs a little pizzazz"? Try these wristers for a special little something extra. Knit in a cotton/silk blend, they won't keep your hands toasty during a snowball fight but they're perfect for texting, shooting pool, playing guitar, or just being your cute self.

Palm

FINISHED MEASUREMENTS
Hand circumference: 7½ (8)"/19 (20.5) cm
Length: 4¾ (5½)"/12 (14) cm

YARN
Deborah Norville Collection Cotton Soft Silk by Premier Yarns, medium worsted weight #4 yarn (78% cotton, 22% silk; 154 yd/3 oz, 141 m/85 g per skein)
• 1 skein #950-06 Emerald

NEEDLES AND OTHER MATERIALS
• US 7 (4.5 mm) set of 5 double-pointed needles (dpns)
• Tapestry needle
• Stitch marker
• Two ½"/1.5 cm buttons

GAUGE
16 sts x 22 rows in St st = 4"/10 cm square
Be sure to check your gauge!

Right Mitt

Back of Hand
CO 8 sts, leaving a 6"/15 cm tail. Divide sts evenly between 4 dpns and join to work in the rnd.
Rnd 1: Knit.
Rnd 2: Kfb in each st to end—16 sts.
Rnd 3: Purl.
Rnd 4: * Yo, k2; rep from * to end—24 sts.
Rnd 5: Knit.
Rnd 6: K2, yo, * k3, yo, rep from * to last st, k1—32 sts.
Rnd 7: Knit.
Rnd 8: * Pfb, p7, rep from * to end—36 sts.
Rnd 9: Purl.
Rnd 10: * K2, m1L, k7, m1R, rep from * to end—44 sts.
Rnd 11: Knit.

Back of hand

Large Size Only

Rnd 12: * K2, m1L, k9, m1R; rep from * around—52 sts.

Rnd 13: Knit.

Both Sizes

Sl first st from Needle 1 to Needle 4, sl first st from Needle 2 to Needle 1, sl first st from Needle 3 to Needle 2, sl first st from Needle 4 to Needle 3—11 (13) sts per needle.

Next rnd: *Needle 1:* BO 11 (13) sts; *Needle 2:* K11 (13); *Needle 3:* BO 11 (13) sts; *Needle 4:* K11 (13)—22 (26) sts rem.

Palm

Rnd 1: *Needle 1:* CO 11 (13) sts using knitted CO; *Needle 2:* K11 (13); *Needle 3:* CO 11 (13) sts; *Needle 4:* K11 (13)—44 (52) sts.

Rnd 2: *Needle 1:* K11 (13); *Needle 2:* K2, BO 5 (7) sts, k4; *Needles 3 & 4:* K11 (13)—11 (13) sts rem on each of needles 1, 3 & 4; 6 sts rem on Needle 2 [2 sts above thumb gap, 4 sts below thumb gap].

Rnd 3: *Needle 1:* K2tog, k7 (9), ssk; *Needle 2:* K2tog, CO 5 (7) sts, k2, ssk; *Needles 3 & 4:* K2tog, k7 (9), ssk—36 (44) sts rem.

Rnd 4: Knit.

Rnd 5: * K2tog, k5 (7), ssk; rep from * to end—28 (36) sts rem.

Rnd 6: Knit.

Rnd 7: * K2tog, k3 (5), ssk; rep from * to end—20 (28) sts rem.

Rnd 8: Knit.

Rnd 9: * K2tog, k1 (3), ssk; rep from * to end—12 (20) sts rem.

Large Size Only

Rnd 10: * K2tog, k1, ssk; rep from * to end—12 sts rem.

Both Sizes

Next rnd: * K2tog, k1; rep from * to end—8 sts rem. Break yarn, thread through tapestry needle and pass through rem live sts. Pull tight, fasten off.

Top Edging

With RS facing, beg at top edge above Thumb, pick up and knit 30 sts evenly around edge. Pm and join to work in the rnd. Purl 1 rnd. Knit 1 rnd. Rep last 2 rnds 1 more time. BO all sts pwise.

Bottom Edging

With RS facing, beg at bottom edge opp Thumb, pick up and knit 30 sts evenly around edge, CO 5 using knitted CO—35 sts. Do not join.

Rnds 1 & 2: Knit.

Rnd 3 (buttonhole row): K1, k2tog, yo, knit to end.

Rnd 4: Knit. BO all sts.

Left Mitt

Back of Hand

Work as for Right Mitt.

Palm

Rnd 1: *Needle 1:* CO 11 (13) sts using knitted CO; *Needle 2:* K11 (13); *Needle 3:* CO 11 (13) sts; *Needle 4:* K11 (13)—44 (52) sts.

Rnd 2: *Needles 1, 2 & 3:* Knit; *Needle 4:* K4, BO 5 (7) sts, k2—11 (13) sts rem on each of needles 1, 2 & 3; 6 sts rem on Needle 4 [2 sts above thumb gap, 4 sts below thumb gap].

Rnd 3: *Needles 1, 2 & 3:* K2tog, k7 (9), ssk; *Needle 4:* K2tog, k2, CO 5 (7) sts, ssk—36 (44) sts rem.

Work remainder of Palm as for Right Mitt.

Top Edging

Work as for Right Mitt.

Bottom Edging

CO 5 sts using knitted CO, with RS facing, beg at bottom edge opp Thumb, pick up and knit 30 sts evenly around edge—35 sts. Do not join.

Rnds 1 & 2: Knit.

Rnd 3 (buttonhole row): Knit to last 3 sts, yo, ssk, k1.

Rnd 4: Knit. BO all sts.

Finishing

Weave in loose ends. Sew button to Bottom Edging underneath Buttonhole.

Make It Yours ✳ Try using a different color for Rnds 1–7 & 10–11 (13) of the Palm for a totally different look!

Gradient Flip-Top Mittens

Apples or oranges, chocolate or vanilla, mittens or fingerless mitts: these are tough decisions that plague us all. With Gradient Flip-Top Mittens, you no longer have to worry about that last one. Need to do some snow shoveling or want to take a long walk on a January evening in Minnesota? No problem, just flip those mitten tops up. Temperatures suddenly moved from subzero to not quite freezing and your hands are getting too warm? No sweat, just unflip the tops and button them down. Worked in natural wool colors and simple patterning, these mittens are suited equally for men and women.

Back of hand

Palm

FINISHED MEASUREMENTS
Hand circumference: 8 (9½)"/20.5 (24) cm
Length: 10 (10¾)"/25.5 (27.5) cm

YARN
Deborah Norville Collection Wool Naturals by Premier Yarns, medium worsted weight #4 yarn (100% wool; 205 yd/3.5 oz, 187 m/100 g per skein)
• 1 skein #425-05 Pewter (A)
• 1 skein #425-03 Sand (B)
• 1 skein #425-01 Cream (C)

NEEDLES AND OTHER MATERIALS

- US 6 (4 mm) set of 5 double-pointed needles (dpns)
- Tapestry needle
- Stitch markers
- Waste yarn
- US E-4 (3.5 mm) crochet hook
- Two ⅝"/1.5 cm buttons

GAUGE

20 sts x 21 rows in stranded knitting = 4"/10 cm square
Be sure to check your gauge!

NOTES

- When working chart rows where there are floats longer than 5 sts, such as Rows 3 and 5, twist the yarn to "trap" the long floats. (See page 112 for a tutorial on stranded knitting.)

STITCH GUIDE

K2, P2 Ribbing (multiple of 4 sts)

Rnd 1: * K2, p2; rep from * to end.
Rep Rnd 1 for patt.

K1, P1 Ribbing (even number of sts)

Rnd 1: * K1, p1; rep from * to end.
Rep Rnd 1 for patt.

Right Mitten

With A, CO 32 (40) sts. Divide sts evenly between 4 dpns and join to work in the rnd.

Cuff

Work in K2, P2 Ribbing for 10 (12) rnds.

Wrist

Setup rnd: * K4 (5), m1L; rep from * to end—40 (48) sts.
Knit 8 (10) rnds.
Work Rows 1–4 of Gradient chart; chart will be repeated 5 (6) times across rnd.

Thumb Gusset

Rnd 1: Work Row 5 of Gradient chart across 22 (26) sts, pm, work Row 1 of Thumb chart, pm, work in patt to end—1 st inc'd.
Rnd 2: Work Row 6 of Gradient chart to m, work Row 2 of Thumb chart, work in patt to end.
Cont in patt through Row 16 of Gradient chart/Row 12 of Thumb chart—13 Thumb sts.
Next rnd: Work Row 17 of Gradient chart to m, place Thumb sts on waste yarn, work in patt to end—40 (48 sts) rem.

Back of hand

Palm

Hand

Cont in patt through Row 27 of Gradient chart. Break B.

Smaller Size Only

Dec rnd: With C, * k2tog, p1, k1, p1; rep from * to end—32 sts rem.

Larger Size Only

Dec rnd: With C, * k2tog, [p1, k1] twice, p2tog, [k1, p1] twice; rep from * to end—40 sts rem.

Both Sizes

Work in K1, P1 Ribbing for 2 rnds. Bind off all sts in patt.

Flip-Top

Locate first st of Row 19 on back of mitten. Hold B inside mitten. Insert crochet hook from RS to inside of mitten, grab loop of yarn, and pull to front—1 st picked up. Working from right to left, pick up 19 (23) more sts along Row 19. Place sts on a dpn. Break yarn.

With B, CO 19 (23) sts, knit across 20 (24) sts from dpn—39 (47) sts. Divide sts between 4 dpns and join to work in the rnd.

Rnd 1: [P1, k1] 9 (11) times, p1, work Row 20 of Gradient chart to end.

Rnd 2: [P1, k1] 9 (11) times, work Row 21 of Gradient chart to end.

Rnd 3: M1L, work Row 22 of Gradient chart across 19 (23) sts, work Row 22 of chart across rem sts—40 (48) sts.

Cont in patt through Row 43 of Gradient chart—5 (6) sts rem. Break yarn, leaving 24" tail, thread through tapestry needle and pass through rem live sts. Fasten off.

Button Loop

With crochet hook, insert hook in Flip-Top 1 st away from tail, sl st to join, ch 8, fasten off. Sew end inside Flip-Top securely.

Thumb

Place held Thumb sts evenly onto 3 dpns. With C, beg at center of Thumb gap, pick up and knit 2 sts (first 2 sts of Thumb chart Row 13), work across Thumb sts in patt, pick up and knit 1st—16 sts.

Work Row 14 of chart—14 sts rem.

Work Rows 15–25 of Thumb chart.

Next rnd: [K3 tog] 4 times, k2tog. Break yarn, thread through tapestry needle, and pass through rem live sts. Fasten off.

Left Mitten

Work as for Right Mitten to Thumb Gusset.

Thumb Gusset

Rnd 1: Work Row 5 of Gradient chart to last 2 sts, pm, work Row 1 of Thumb chart, pm, work in patt to end—1 st inc'd.

Rnd 2: Work Row 6 of Gradient chart to m, work Row 2 of Thumb chart, work in patt to end.

Cont in patt through Row 18 of Gradient chart/Row 12 of Thumb chart—13 Thumb sts.

Next rnd: Work Row 19 of Gradient chart to m, place Thumb sts on waste yarn, work in patt to end—40 (48 sts) rem.

Comp as for Right Mitten.

Finishing

Weave in loose ends. Fold back Flip-Top. Position button underneath Button Loop; sew in place.

Gradient

Key

- ☐ knit
- ■ A
- ▨ B
- ☐ C
- ◪ k2tog
- ◨ ssk
- ☒ no st
- L make 1 left
- R make 1 right
- ☐ patt rep

Thumb

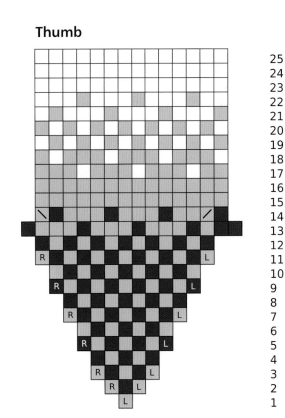

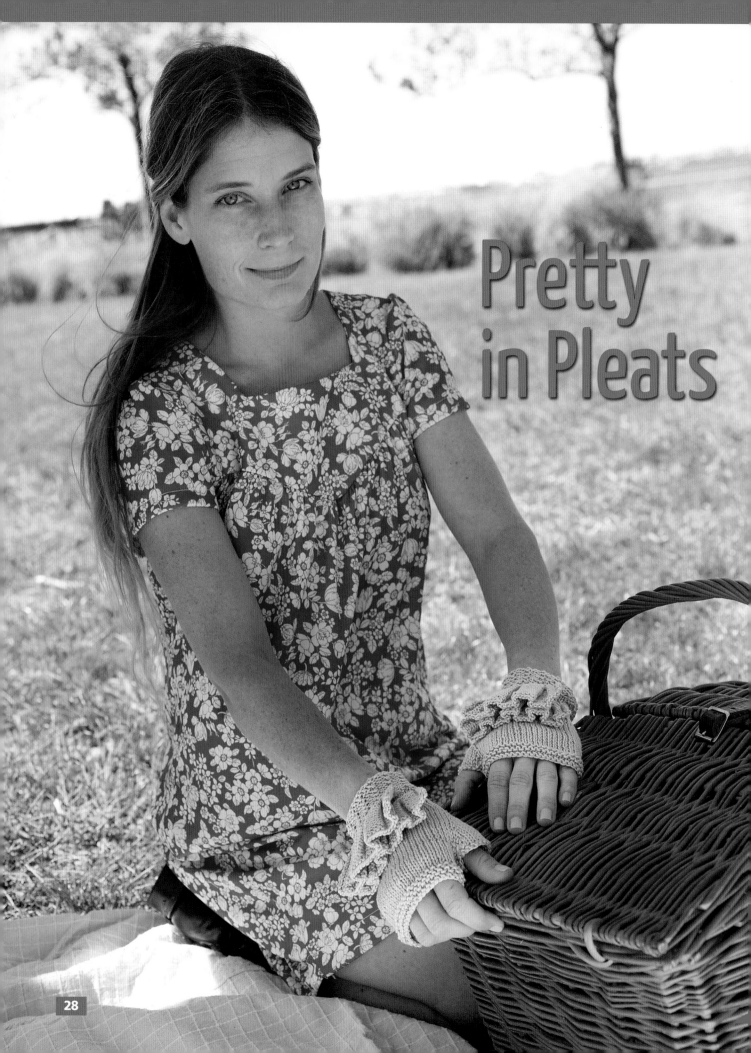

Pretty
in Pleats

I f you've ever sewn a pleat, the pleated technique in this pattern will make perfect sense to you. If not, no worries! I've included a photo tutorial for you on pages 116–118.

FINISHED MEASUREMENTS
Hand circumference: 7 (7¾, 8¼)"/18 (19.5, 21) cm
Length: 6 (6½, 7)"/15 (16.5, 18) cm (not including pleats)

YARN
Premier Yarns Afternoon Cotton, DK weight #3 yarn (100% Egyptian Giza mercerized cotton; 136 yd/1.75 oz, 124 m/50 g per skein)
• 1 skein #22-07 Lavender

NEEDLES AND OTHER MATERIALS
• US 3 (3.25 mm) set of 5 double-pointed needles (dpn)
• 2 cable needles or spare dpns
• Tapestry needle
• Stitch markers
• Waste yarn

GAUGE
23 sts x 32 rows in St st = 4"/10 cm square
Be sure to check your gauge!

NOTES
• When casting on for the Thumb Gusset, use the backward-loop method (see page 103 for a tutorial).

STITCH GUIDE
Box Pleat
This technique will resemble a sewn pleat, where the fabric is folded accordion style. This pleat is worked over 12 stitches. (See page 116 for full step-by-step instructions with photos.)

First Half of Pleat
Slip the first 2 stitches on the left needle to a spare dpn or cable needle; hold this dpn in back of the work. Slip the next 2 stitches on the left needle to a second dpn. Rotate this dpn clockwise 180 degrees and hold it between the left needle and the first dpn. Insert the needle through the front leg of the first stitch on each needle and knit these three stitches together (k3tog). K3tog once more with the second stitch on each needle—2 stitches on the right needle.

(continued on next page)

Second Half of Pleat

Slip the first 2 stitches on the left needle to a dpn and hold in front of the work. Slip the next 2 stitches on the left needle to a second dpn. Rotate this dpn counterclockwise 180 degrees and hold between the left needle and the first dpn. K3tog twice. One box pleat completed.

Right Mitt

CO 39 (42, 45) sts. Divide evenly among 4 dpns and join to work in the rnd.

Cuff

Rnd 1: * K1 tbl, p2; rep from * to end.
Rnd 2: Purl.
Rep Rnds 1 & 2 five more times, then rep Rnd 1 one more time.

Hand

7"/18 cm Size Only
Inc rnd: Kfb, knit to end—40 sts.

7³⁄₄"/19.5 cm Size Only
Inc rnd: * Kfb, k20; rep from * once more—44 sts.

8¹⁄₄"/21 cm Size Only
Inc rnd: * Kfb, k14; rep from * 2 more times—48 sts.

All Sizes
Next rnd: K2 (3, 4), p16, knit to end. The 16 purl bumps on this rnd indicate where to sew Lower Pleat.
Knit 4 rnds.
Next rnd: K0 (1, 2), p20, knit to end. The 20 purl bumps on this rnd indicate where to sew Upper Pleat.
Knit 2 rnds.

Thumb Gusset

Rnd 1: K22 (24, 26), pm, m1L, pm, knit to end—1 st inc'd.
Rnd 2: Knit.
Rnd 3: Knit to m, sl m, CO 1 st, knit to m, CO 1 st, knit to end—2 sts inc'd.
Rnd 4: Knit.
Rep last 2 rnds 7 (8, 9) more times—17 (19, 21) Thumb sts.
Next rnd: Knit to marker, place Thumb sts on waste yarn, knit to end—40 (44, 48) sts rem.
Knit 8 (10, 12) rnds.
Next rnd: Purl.
Next rnd: Knit.
Rep these 2 rnds 1 more time. BO all sts pwise.

Thumb

Place held Thumb sts evenly onto 3 dpns. Beg at center of Thumb gap, pick up and knit 2 sts, k17 (19, 21), pick up and knit 1—20 (22, 24) sts.
Dec rnd: K1, k2tog, knit to last 2 sts, ssk—18 (20, 22) sts rem. BO all sts loosely pwise.

Lower Pleat

CO 40 sts.
Rows 1 & 2: Knit.
Row 3 (RS): P1, knit to last st, p1.
Row 4: K1, purl to last st, k1.
Rows 5–14: Rep Rows 3 & 4.
Row 15: P1, k1, * Box Pleat; rep from * to last 2 sts, k1, p1 —16 sts rem.
Knit 2 rows. BO all sts over next WS row, leaving 12" tail.

Upper Pleat

CO 52 sts.
Rows 1 & 2: Knit.
Row 3 (RS): P1, knit to last st, p1.
Row 4: K1, purl to last st, k1.
Rows 5–10: Rep Rows 3 & 4.
Row 11: P1, k1, * Box Pleat; rep from * to last 2 sts, k1, p1 —20 sts rem.
Knit 2 rows. BO all sts over next WS row, leaving 12" tail.

Left Mitt

Work as for Right Mitt to Thumb Gusset.

Thumb Gusset

Rnd 1: Knit to last 2 sts, pm, m1L, pm, knit to end—1 st inc'd.
Comp as for Right Mitt. Make Lower and Upper Pleats as for Right Mitt.

Finishing

Sew BO edge of Lower Pleat to mitt using whipstitch.
Rep for Upper Pleat. Weave in loose ends.

Smartgloves

A smarter way to email, text, and browse the internet, Smartgloves are here to keep your hands warm and still allow you to pinch the screen of your smartphone. The pattern is written to accommodate the right-handed. For the lefties out there, simply make a full thumb and index finger for your right glove, and follow instructions for the half thumb and index finger for your left glove.

FINISHED MEASUREMENTS
Hand circumference: 7 (8¼)"/18 (21) cm
Length: 9¼ (10½)"/23.5 (26.5) cm

YARN
Deborah Norville Collection Serenity Sock Solids by Premier Yarns, superfine weight #1 yarn (50% superwash merino wool, 25% rayon from bamboo, 25% nylon; 230 yd/1.75 oz, 210 m/50 g per skein)
• 1 skein #150-11 Charcoal

Smartgloves Chart

Key

☐	knit
●	yo
b	k1 tbl
⬚	LKPC
⬚	RKPC
⬚	LC
⬚	RC
⬚	LPC
⬚	RPC

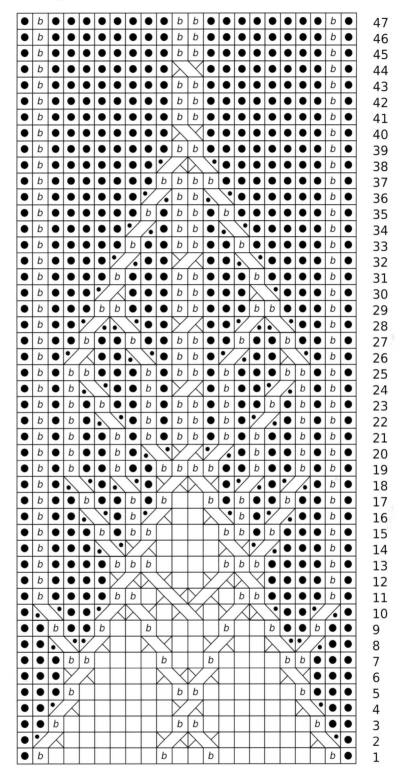

NEEDLES AND OTHER MATERIALS
- US 1 (2.25 mm) set of 5 double-pointed needles (dpns)
- 4 spare US 1 (2.25 mm) or smaller dpns
- Cable needle
- Tapestry needle
- Stitch markers
- Waste yarn

GAUGE
30 sts x 44 rows in St st = 4"/10 cm square
Be sure to check your gauge!

STITCH GUIDE
Left Knit Purl Cross (LKPC)
Sl next st to cn and hold in front, p1, k1 from cn.

Right Knit Purl Cross (RKPC)
Sl next st to cn and hold in back, k1, p1 from cn.

Left Cross (LC)
Sl next st to cn and hold in front, k1, k1 from cn.

Right Cross (RC)
Sl next st to cn and hold in back, k1, k1 from cn.

Left Purl Cross (LPC)
Work as for LKPC.

Right Purl Cross (RPC)
Work as for RKPC.

Right Twist (RT)
Skip next st on LH needle and knit 2nd st (do not remove from needle), then knit skipped st, then sl both sts from needle.

> **TIP *** RKPC and RPC are worked in the same manner; however, they have different symbols in the chart because they are worked over different stitches. (A RKPC begins when the next two stitches are both knit stitches; a RPC begins when the next two stitches are a knit and a purl.) The same is true for LKPC and LPC.

Right Glove

Thumb
CO 20 (22) sts. Divide evenly between 3 dpns and join to work in the rnd. Knit every rnd until Thumb measures 2½ (2¾)"/6.5 (7) cm. Break yarn. Place sts on 2 spare dpns.

Pinky Finger
CO 7 (8) sts, leaving 6"/15 cm tail. Divide evenly between 3 dpns and join to work in the rnd. Knit 1 rnd.
Next rnd: Kfb to end—14 (16) sts.
Knit every rnd until Pinky measures 2¼ (2½)"/5.5 (6.5) cm. Slip first 7 (8) sts onto a spare dpn and last 7 (8) sts onto another spare dpn. Break yarn.

Ring Finger
CO 8 (9) sts, leaving 6"/15 cm tail. Divide evenly among 3 dpns and join to work in the rnd. Knit 1 rnd.
Next rnd: Kfb to end—16 (18) sts.
Knit every rnd until Ring Finger measures 2¾ (3)"/7 (7.5) cm. Slip first 8 (9) sts onto the dpn next to first 7 (8) Pinky sts and last 8 (9) sts onto other dpn next to last 7 (8) Pinky sts. Break yarn.

Middle Finger
Work as for Ring Finger until Middle Finger measures 3¼ (3½)"/8 (9) cm. Slip first 8 (9) sts onto dpn next to first 8 (9) Ring Finger sts and last 8 (9) sts onto other dpn next to last 8 (9) Ring Finger sts. Break yarn.

Index Finger
CO 16 (18) sts. Divide evenly among 3 dpns and join to work in the rnd. Knit every rnd until Index Finger measures 2¼ (2½)"/5.5 (6.5) cm. Do not break yarn.

Join Fingers
Next rnd: Knit to last st 2 sts of Index Finger, ssk; working across first Middle Finger sts, k2tog, k4 (5), ssk; working across Ring Finger, k2tog, k4 (5), ssk; working across Pinky, ssk, k10 (12), k2tog; working across rem Ring Finger sts, k2tog, k4 (5), ssk; working across rem Middle Finger sts, k2tog, k4 (5), ssk; working across rem Index Finger sts, k2tog, k6 (7), pm for beg of rnd—50 (58) sts.

Hand
Knit 1 (5) rnds.
Next rnd: K1 (3), pm, work Row 1 of chart across 22 sts, pm, knit to end.
Next rnd: Knit to m, work Row 2 of chart to m, knit to end.
Cont in patt through Row 19 of chart.

Thumb Gusset

Next rnd: Knit to m, work Row 20 of chart to m, knit to last 4 sts, pm, k1, k20 (22) Thumb sts, k1, pm, knit to end—70 (80) sts.

Next rnd: Knit to m, work next row of chart to m, knit to end.

Cont to work even in patt for 2 (4) more rnds,

Dec rnd: Knit to m, work next row of chart to m, knit to Thumb m, ssk, knit to 2 sts bef m, k2tog, knit to end—2 sts dec'd.

Next rnd: Knit to m, work next row of chart to m, knit to end.

Rep last 2 rnds 9 (10) more times—50 (58) sts rem, 2 sts rem between Thumb markers. Remove Thumb markers. Last row of chart just worked was 43 (47).

Larger Size

On Row 47 of chart, work to last st of hand, place this st on LH needle. This is the new beg of rnd.

Cuff

Setup rnd: [P1, RT] 3 (4) times, p2tog, RT, p2tog, [RT, p1] 4 times, RT, p2tog, [RT, p1] to last 4 sts, RT, p2tog—46 (54) sts rem.

Rnd 1: K2tog, k1 tbl, p1, * [k1 tbl] twice, p1; rep from * to end—45 (54) sts rem.

Rnd 2: * [K1 tbl] twice, p1; rep from * to end.

Rnd 3: Rep Rnd 2.

Rnd 4: * RT, p1; rep from * to end.

Rnd 5: Rep Rnd 2.

Rep Rnds 2–5 three (four) more times. Knit 3 rnds. BO all sts loosely.

Left Glove

Thumb

CO 10 (11) sts, leaving 6" tail. Divide evenly between 3 dpns and join to work in the rnd. Knit 1 rnd.

Next rnd: Kfb to end—20 (22) sts.

Knit every rnd until Thumb measures 2¼ (2½)"/5.5 (6.5) cm. Break yarn. Place sts on 2 spare dpns.

Pinky Finger, Ring Finger, Middle Finger

Work as for Right Glove

Index Finger

CO 8 (9) sts. Divide evenly between 3 dpns and join to work in the rnd.

Next rnd: Kfb to end—16 (18) sts.

Knit every rnd until Index Finger measures 2¼ (2½)"/5.5 (6.5) cm. Do not break yarn.

Join Fingers

Work as for Right hand through Rnd 19 of chart.

Thumb Gusset

Next rnd: Knit to m, work Row 20 of chart to m, k4 (6), pm, k1, k20 (22) Thumb sts, k1, pm, knit to end—70 (80) sts.

Next rnd: K1 (3), work next row of chart to m, knit to end.

Cont to work even in patt for 2 (4) more rnds,

Dec rnd: Knit to m, work next row of chart to m, knit to Thumb m, ssk, knit to 2 sts bef m, k2tog, knit to end—2 sts dec'd.

Next rnd: Knit to m, work next row of chart to m, knit to end.

Rep last 2 rnds, 9 (10) more times—50 (58) sts rem, 2 sts rem between Thumb markers. Remove Thumb markers. Last row of chart just worked was 43 (47).

Larger Size

On Row 47 of chart, work to last st of hand, place this st on LH needle. This is the new beg of rnd.

Cuff

Setup rnd: [P1, RT] 3 (4) times, p2tog, RT, p2tog, [RT, p1] 4 times, RT, p2tog, [RT, p1] to last 4 sts, RT, p2tog—46 (54) sts rem.

Rnd 1: K2tog, k1 tbl, p1, * [k1 tbl] twice, p1; rep from * to end—45 (54) sts rem.

Rnd 2: * [K1 tbl] twice, p1; rep from * to end.

Rnd 3: Rep Rnd 2.

Rnd 4: * RT, p1; rep from * to end.

Rnd 5: Rep Rnd 2.

Rep Rnds 2–5 three (four) more times. Knit 3 rnds. BO all sts loosely.

Finishing

Using yarn ends, sew up holes bet fingers and at tips of full fingers and thumb. Sew thumb gap closed. Weave in loose ends. Wet block to even out knitting.

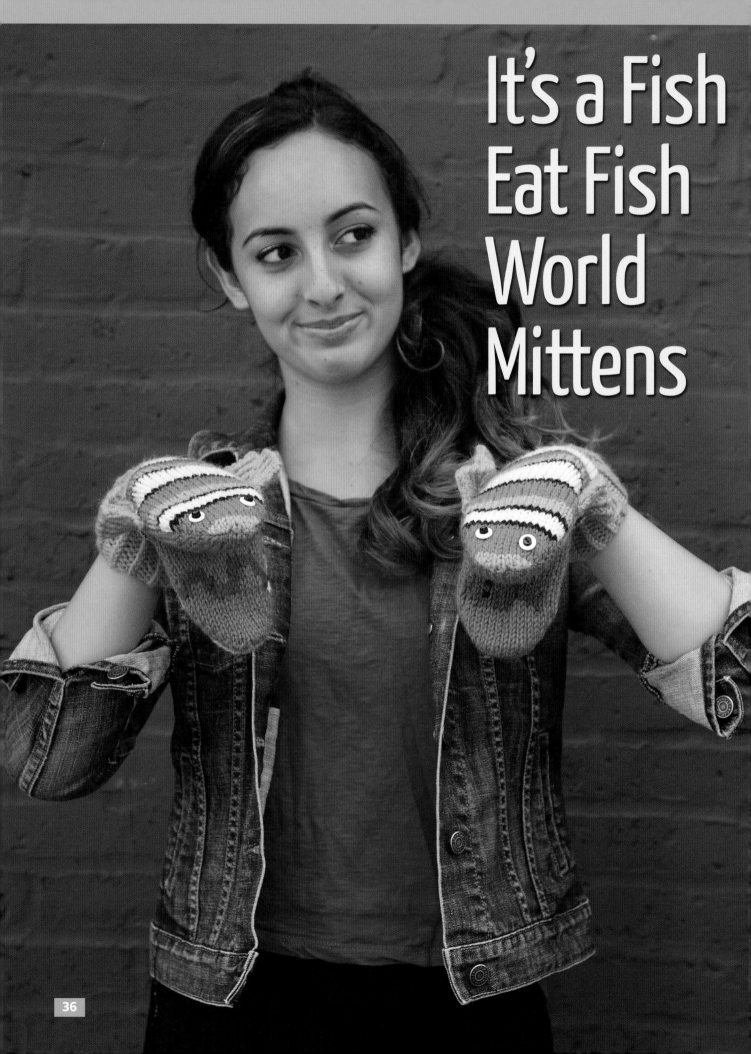

It's a Fish Eat Fish World Mittens

These adorable mittens are constructed like puppets and are both fun and functional. The extra room in the thumb provides additional warmth for those days when you need something both warm and quirky. As written, the mittens eat a fish on one hand and a worm on the other. Want your fish to eat something different? Be creative; make up your own fish food!

FINISHED MEASUREMENTS
Hand circumference: 7"/18 cm
Length: 9"/23 cm

YARN
Premier Yarns Wool Worsted, medium worsted weight #4 yarn (100% wool; 186 yd/3.5 oz, 170 m/100 g per skein)
- 1 skein #35-107 Orange Peel (A)
- 1 skein #35-115 True Black (B)
- 1 skein #35-101 Cream (C)
- 1 skein #35-108 Tangerine (D)
- 1 skein #35-119 Mermaid (E)
- 1 skein #35-120 Raspberry

NEEDLES AND OTHER MATERIALS
- US 6 (4 mm) set of 5 double-pointed needles (dpns)
- Tapestry needle
- Sewing needle and thread
- Four ½"/1.5 cm white buttons
- Four ¼"/.5 cm black buttons
- Stitch holder

GAUGE
18 sts x 24 rows in St st = 4"/10 cm square
Be sure to check your gauge!

NOTES
- When working Fish Stripes, carry unused strands loosely up the side of the work. Do not cut yarn at the end of a stripe. Depending on the position of the yarn when it comes time to use it, you may have to slide your sts to other end of dpn and purl or knit more than one row in succession in order to maintain St st.

STITCH GUIDE
Twisted Rib (odd number of sts)
Row 1: K1, * p1tbl, k1tbl; rep from * to last 2 sts, p1tbl, k1.
Row 2: P1, * k1tbl, p1tbl; rep from * to last 2 sts, k1tbl, p1.
Rep Rows 1 & 2 for patt.

Body

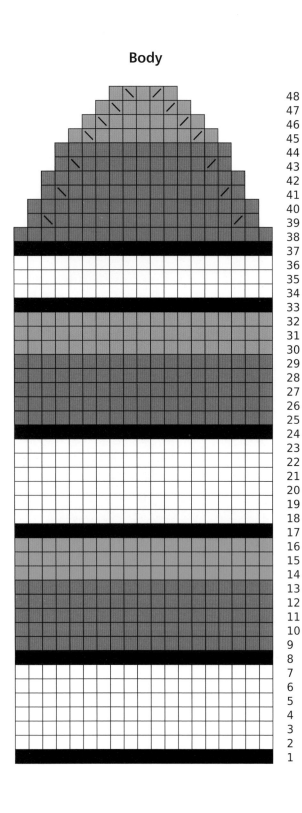

Key

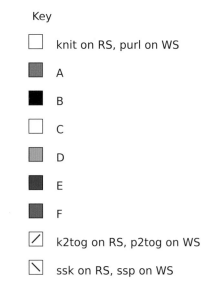

knit on RS, purl on WS

A

B

C

D

E

F

k2tog on RS, p2tog on WS

ssk on RS, ssp on WS

Upper Mouth

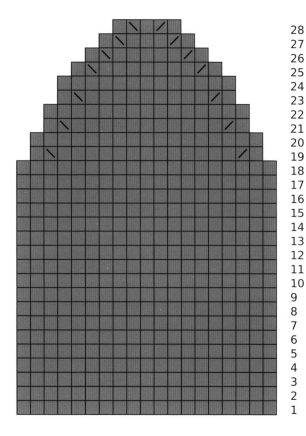

Right Mitten

With A, CO 45 sts. Divide evenly between 4 dpns and join to work in the rnd.

Tail

Rnds 1–9: * K1tbl, p2; rep from * to end.
Rnd 10: * [K1tbl, p2tog]; rep from * to end—30 sts rem.
Rnds 11–13: * K1tbl, p1; rep from * to end.
Rnd 14: * K7, m1L, k8, m1L; rep from * once more—34 sts.

Body

With B, CO 1 st, k17 (Row 1 of Body chart), CO 1 st, place rem 17 sts on holder for Bottom of Fish; 19 sts rem for Top of Fish.

Top of Fish

Remainder of Hand is knit back and forth in rows.
Work Rows 2-48 of Body chart. BO rem sts.

Bottom of Fish

Place held sts on needle and attach B.
Row 1 (RS): CO 1 st, k17 (Row 1 of Body chart), CO 1 st—19 sts. Comp as for Top of Fish.

Fish Mouth, Lower

With D, CO 19 sts. Work Rows 1–28 of Poor Little Fish chart.
Note: Instead of working the 2 black "eye" sts as you knit the Mouth, you may wish to embroider these on after the Mouth is complete.
BO rem sts.

Fish Mouth, Upper

With D and RS facing, pick up and knit 19 sts from CO edge of Lower Fish Mouth (this counts as Row 1 of Upper Mouth chart). Work Rows 2–28 of Upper Mouth chart. BO rem sts.

Right Fin

CO 25 sts.
Row 1: Work Row 1 of Twisted Rib.
Row 2: Work in Twisted Rib across 8 sts, sl 2, k1, p2sso, work in Twisted Rib to end—23 sts rem.
Row 3: Work in patt across 13 sts, [p1 tbl] 3 times, work in patt to end.
Row 4: Work in patt across 7 sts, sl 2, k1, p2sso, work in patt to end—21 sts rem.
Row 5: Work even in patt.

Poor Little Fish

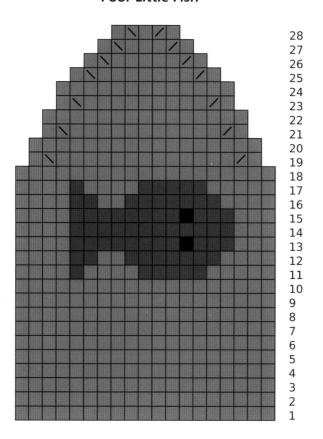

Unfortunate Worm

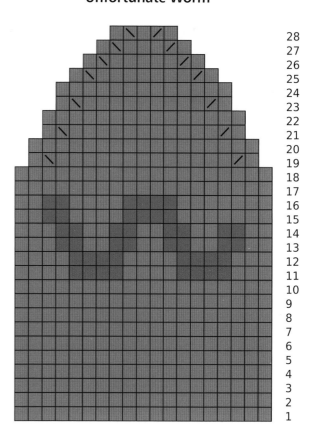

Row 6: Work in patt across 6 sts, sl 2, k1, p2sso, work in patt to end—19 sts rem.

BO rem sts in patt.

Left Fin

CO 25 sts.

Row 1: Work Row 1 of Twisted Rib.

Row 2: Work in Twisted Rib across 14 sts, sl 2, k1, p2sso, work in Twisted Rib to end—23 sts rem.

Row 3: Work in patt across 7 sts, [p1 tbl] 3 times, work in patt to end.

Row 4: Work in patt across 13 sts, sl 2, k1, p2sso, work in Twisted Rib to end—21 sts rem.

Row 5: Work even in patt.

Row 6: Work in patt across 11 sts, sl 2, k1, p2sso, work in patt to end—19 sts rem.

BO rem sts in patt.

Left Mitten

Work as for Right Mitten, substituting Unfortunate Worm chart for Poor Little Fish chart.

Finishing

Layer a black button on top of a white button. Sew to Top of fish for eye. Rep for other 3 eyes.

Sew sides of Top and Bottom of Fish tog along approx 3" from Row 1 to Row 20.

Weave in ends.

Place Mouth into Fish Body, wrong sides tog. Sew edges tog around entire perimeter using mattress stitch.

Sew BO edge of Fins to respective Right and Left sides of Fish, with top edge of each Fin approx 3" 7.5 cm from tip of mitten.

Weave in loose ends. Eat some big fish.

Purple
Pixie

These whimsical mitts are a lot of fun to make! Each pointed cuff is worked separately from the bottom up. Don't let the large cast-on number throw you off. Stitches are decreased every other round, leaving you with a more manageable number in no time. Be sure to wear these while flying through the woods, climbing trees, making mischief, or anything else a pixie might do!

FINISHED MEASUREMENTS
Hand circumference: 7 (8)"/18 (20.5 cm)
Length: 9½"/24 cm

YARN
Premier Yarns Cotton Fair, fine weight #2 yarn (52% cotton, 48% acrylic; 317 yd/3.5 oz, 805 m/ 100 g per skein)
• 1 skein #2709 Lavender

NEEDLES AND OTHER MATERIALS
• US 3 (3.25 mm) set of 5 double-pointed needles (dpns)
• 4 spare US 3 (3.25 mm) or smaller dpns
• Tapestry needle
• Stitch markers
• Waste yarn

GAUGE
24 sts x 30 rows in St st = 4"/10 cm square
Be sure to check your gauge!

Right Mitt

Upper Cuff
CO 114 (120) sts. Divide evenly between 4 dpns and join to work in the rnd.
Rnd 1: Purl.
Rnd 2: * K16 (17), sl2, k1, p2sso; rep from * to end—102 (108) sts rem.
Rnd 3: * P16 (17), k1; rep from * to end.
Rnd 4: K15 (16), sl 2, k1, p2sso, * k14 (15), sl 2, k1, p2sso; rep from * to last 16 (17) sts, k14 (15), sl 2, k1 (first st of this rnd), p2sso—90 (96) sts rem.
Rnd 5: Knit.
Rnd 6: K13 (14), sl 2, k1, p2sso, * k12 (13), sl 2, k1, p2sso; rep from * to last 14 (15) sts, k12 (13), sl 2, k1 (first st of this rnd), p2sso—78 (84) sts rem.
Rnd 7: * P12 (13), k1; rep from * to end.

Rnd 8: K11 (12), sl 2, k1, p2sso, * k10 (11), sl 2, k1, p2sso; rep from * to last 12 (13) sts, k10 (11), sl 2, k1 (first st of this rnd), p2sso—66 (72) sts rem.
Rnd 9: Knit.
Rnd 10: K9 (10), sl 2, k1, p2sso, * k8 (9), sl 2, k1, p2sso; rep from * to last 10 (11) sts, k8 (9), sl 2, k1 (first st of this rnd), p2sso—54 (60) sts rem,
Rnd 11: Knit.
Rnd 12: K7 (8), sl 2, k1, p2sso, * k6 (7), sl 2, k1, p2sso; rep from * to last 8 (9) sts, k6 (7), sl 2, k1 (first st of this rnd), p2sso—42 (48) sts rem.
Break yarn, place sts evenly on 4 spare dpns.

Lower Cuff

CO 114 (120) sts. Divide evenly between 4 dpns and join to work in the rnd.

Rnd 1: Purl.

Rnd 2: K8, sl 2, k1, p2sso, * k16 (17), sl2, k1, p2sso; rep from * 5 times, knit to end—102 (108) sts rem.

Rnd 3: P8, k1, * p16 (17), k1; rep from * 5 times, purl to end.

Rnd 4: K7, sl 2, k1, p2sso, * k14 (15), sl2, k1, p2sso; rep from * 5 times, knit to end—90 (96) sts rem.

Rnd 5: Knit.

Rnd 6: K6, sl 2, k1, p2sso, * k12 (13), sl2, k1, p2sso; rep from * 5 times, knit to end—78 (84) sts rem.

Rnd 7: P6, k1, * p12 (13), k1; rep from * 5 times, knit to end.

Rnd 8: K5, sl 2, k1, p2sso, * k10 (11), sl2, k1, p2sso; rep from * 5 times, knit to end—66 (72) sts rem.

Rnd 9: Knit.

Rnd 10: K4, sl 2, k1, p2sso, * k8 (9), sl2, k1, p2sso; rep from * 5 times, knit to end—54 (60) sts rem.

Rnd 11: Knit.

Rnd 12: K3, sl 2, k1, p2sso, * k6 (7), sl2, k1, p2sso; rep from * 5 times, knit to end—42 (48) sts rem.

Knit 10 rnds.

Next rnd: * K1, p1; rep from * to end. Rep this rnd, 5 more times.

Wrist

Place Upper Cuff around Lower Cuff, so that Upper Cuff needles are parallel to Lower Cuff needles, and on the outside.

Joining rnd: * Knit 1 st from Upper Cuff tog with 1 st from Lower Cuff; rep from * to end—42 (48) sts.

Next rnd: * P6 (7), k1; rep from * to end. Rep this rnd, 12 times.

Thumb Gusset

Rnd 1: Work in patt to last 8 (9) sts, pm, kfb, pm, work in patt to end—1 st inc'd.

Rnd 2: Work in patt to m, k2, work in patt to end.

Rnd 3: Work in patt to m, k1, m1P, k1, work in patt to end—1 st inc'd.

Rnd 4: Work in patt to m, k1, m1P, purl to 1 st bef m, m1P, k1, work in patt to end—2 sts inc'd.

Rnd 5: Work in patt to m, k1, purl to 1 st bef m, k1, work in patt to end.

Rep last 2 rnds 8 (9) more times—21 (23) Thumb sts.

Hand

Next rnd: Work in patt to m, sl m, k1, p1, slip Thumb sts to waste yarn, p1, k1, work in patt to end—42 (48) sts rem.

Next rnd: Work in patt to m, k1, p2, k1, work in patt to end.

Next rnd: Work in patt to m, ssk, k2tog, work in patt to end—2 sts dec'd.

Next rnd: Work in patt to m, remove m, k2tog, remove m, work in patt to end—42 (48) sts rem.

Work even in patt for ¾"/2 cm. Purl 1 rnd. Knit 2 rnds. Purl 1 rnd. Knit 1 rnd. Purl 1 rnd. BO all sts, pwise.

Thumb

Place held Thumb sts evenly on 3 dpns. Beg at center of Thumb gap, pick up and purl 2 sts, p21 (23), pick up and purl 1—24 (26) sts.

Dec rnd: P1, p2tog, purl to last 3 sts, p2tog, p1—22 (24) sts rem.

Purl 2 rnds. Knit 1 rnd. BO all sts loosely pwise.

Left Mitt

Work as for Right Mitt to Thumb Gusset.

Thumb Gusset

Rnd 1: Work in patt across 6 (7) sts, pm, kfb, pm, work in patt to end—1 st inc'd.

Comp as for Right Mitt.

Finishing

Weave in loose ends.

Sunstreak

ntarsia in the round? Yep, that's right. Sunstreak Mitts are worked entirely in the round with the "streaks" worked at the same time. Before beginning, cut lengths of color A for the second and third streak, and use the yarn coming from the ball for the first streak. The movement in the streaks is caused by working simple 1x1 crosses; be sure the A stitch is always crossed over the B stitch. For a more subtle-looking mitt, try using tonal colors or colors with similar values for A and B.

Back of hand

Palm

FINISHED MEASUREMENTS
Hand circumference: 7¾ (8¾)"/19.5 (22 cm)
Length: 7¼ (8½)"/18.5 (21.5 cm)

YARN
Deborah Norville Collection Cotton Soft Silk by Premier Yarns, medium worsted #4 yarn (78% cotton, 22% silk; 152 yd/3 oz, 139 m/85 g per skein)
• 1 skein #950-02 Tangerine (A)
Deborah Norville Collection Cotton Soft Silk Multis by Premier Yarns, medium worsted #4 yarn (78% cotton, 22% silk; 126 yd/2.5 oz, 115 m/71 g per skein)
• 1 skein #955-04 Undersea Treasure (B)

NEEDLES AND OTHER MATERIALS
• US 6 (4 mm) set of 5 double-pointed needles (dpns)
• US 7 (4.5 mm) set of 5 dpns
• Tapestry needle
• Stitch markers
• Waste yarn

GAUGE
Using larger needles, 18 sts x 24 rows in St st = 4"/10 cm
square
Be sure to check your gauge!

NOTES
• In Sunstreak Pattern, the "streaks" of color A are
worked using a modified intarsia method. Work up
to the A stitch, drop the B yarn, work the A stitch,
drop the A yarn, bring the B strand from beneath the
A strand, and continue working. Do not twist strands.

STITCH GUIDE
Left Cross (LC)
Sl next A st off needle and drop to front of work, sl next B
st, place A st back on LH needle, sl next B st back to LH
needle, p1 with B, k1 with A.

Right Cross (RC)
Slip next B st, sl next A st off needle and drop to front
of work, sl B st back to LH needle, place A st back on LH
needle, k1 with A, p1 with B.

Sunstreak Pattern (worked over 15 sts)
Setup row: With A, k1, with B, p4, * adding in new
strand of A, k1, with B, p4; rep from * once more.
Row 1: * LC, with B, p3; rep from * 2 more times.
Row 2: With B, p1, LC, with B, p2; rep from * 2 more
times.
Row 3: With B, p2, LC, with B, p1; rep from * 2 more
times.
Row 4: With B, p3, LC; rep from * 2 more times.
Row 5: With B, p2, RC, with B, p1; rep from * 2 more
times.
Row 6: With B, p1, RC, with B, p2; rep from * 2 more
times.
Row 7: RC, with B, p3; rep from * 2 more times.
Rep Rows 1-7 for patt.

Right Mitt

Cut 2 strands of A 54 (72)" / 137 (183) cm long. Set aside
for Hand.
With A and smaller needles, CO 32 (36) sts. Divide evenly
between 4 dpns and join to work in the rnd.

Cuff
Rnds 1–6: * K1, p1; rep from * to end,
Rnds 7–9: * K1, p3; rep from * to end.
Inc rnd: [K4, m1L] 3 times, knit to end—35 (39) sts.

Hand
Switch to larger needles.
Setup rnd: Work setup row of Sunstreak patt across 15
sts, pm, with B, p10 (12). Pm for new beg of rnd.
Rnd 1: With B, p10 (12), work row 1 of Sunstreak patt to
m, with B purl to end.
Rnds 2–7 (10): Work even in patt, ending with Row 7 (3)
of patt.

Thumb Gusset
Inc rnd: P10 (12), work in patt to m, p2 (4), pm for
Thumb, m1p, pm for Thumb, purl to end—1 st inc'd.
Next rnd: Work in patt to Thumb m, purl to end.
Inc rnd: Work in patt to Thumb m, m1p, purl to m, m1p,
purl to end—2 sts inc'd.
Next rnd: Work in patt to Thumb m, purl to end.
Rep last 2 rnds 4 (5) more times—11 (13) Thumb sts.
Work 2 rnds even in patt.
Next rnd: Work in patt to Thumb m, place Thumb sts on
waste yarn, work in patt to end—35 (39) sts rem.
Cont in patt for 6 (8) more rnds, ending with Row 7 of
patt.
Next rnd: Purl to m, * with A, k1, with B, p4; rep from *
2 more times, p10 (12). This is new beg of rnd. Break B.

Top Edging
Rnd 1: With A, knit.
Rnd 2: [K1, p2, p2tog] 3 times, * k1, p3; rep from * to end
—32 (36) sts rem.
Rnds 3 & 4: * K1, p3; rep from * to end.
BO all sts loosely in patt.

Thumb
Place Thumb sts evenly on 3 dpns. Beg at center of Thumb
gap, pick up and knit 2 sts, p11 (13), pick up and knit
1 st—14 (16) sts.
Dec rnd: P1, P2tog, purl to last 3 sts, p2tog, p1—12 (14)
sts rem. BO all sts loosely, kwise.

Left Mitt

Work as for Right Mitt to Thumb Gusset.

Thumb Gusset
Inc rnd: P8, pm for Thumb, m1p, pm for Thumb, p2 (4),
work in patt to end—1 st inc'd.
Comp as for Right Mitt

Finishing

Weave in loose ends.

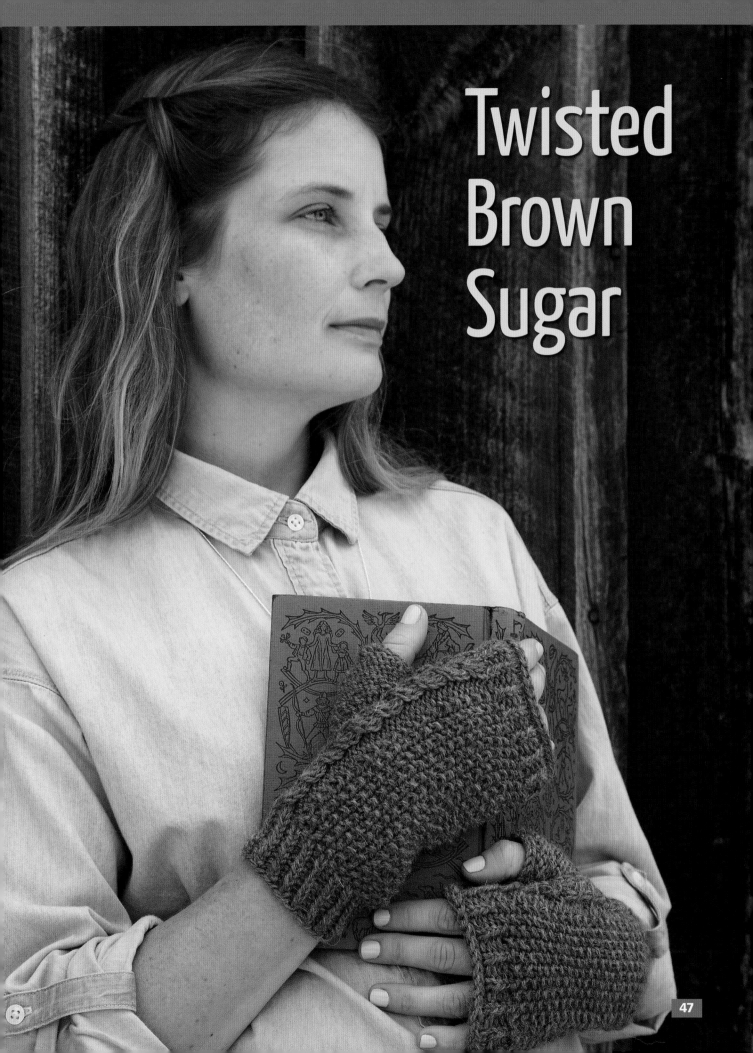

Twisted Brown Sugar

Cables, texture, and wool go together like PB&J, no? Worked in a worsted weight rustic-feeling wool, these classic mitts will fly off your needles in no time. Delicate twisted cables run parallel along the interior wrist, part ways around the thumb gusset, and then come back together again at the top of the hand.

FINISHED MEASUREMENTS
Hand circumference: 7 (8)"/18 (20.5) cm
Length: 7½ (8)"/19 (20.5) cm

YARN
Deborah Norville Wool Naturals by Premier Yarns, medium worsted #4 yarn (100% wool; 205 yd/3.5 oz, 187 m/ 100 g per skein)
• 1 skein #425-04 Slate

NEEDLES AND OTHER MATERIALS
• US 6 (4 mm) set of 5 double-pointed needles (dpns)
• Tapestry needle
• Stitch markers
• Waste yarn

GAUGE
18 sts x 28 rows in Seed St = 4"/10 cm square
Be sure to check your gauge!

STITCH GUIDE
Twisted Rib (even number of sts)
Rnd 1: * K1 tbl, p1; rep from * to end.
Rep Rnd 1 for patt.

Seed Stitch (Seed St) (odd number of sts)
Row 1: * P1, k1; rep from * to last st, p1.
Row 2: * K1, p1; rep from * to last st, k1.
Rep Rows 1 and 2 for patt.

Seed Stitch (even number of sts)
Row 1: * P1, k1; rep from * to end.
Row 2: * K1, p1; rep from * to end.
Rep Rows 1 and 2 for patt.

Twisted Panel Right (worked over 3 sts)
Rows 1, 3 & 4: Knit.
Row 2: Tw-R.
Rep Rows 1-4 for patt.

Twisted Panel Left (worked over 3 sts)
Rows 1, 3 & 4: Knit.
Row 2: Tw-L.
Rep Rows 1-4 for patt.

Twist Right (tw-R)
Knit 3rd st on LH needle, then knit 2nd st on LH needle, then knit 1st st on LH needle; sl all 3 sts from needle.

Twist Left (tw-L)
Working from behind, knit 3rd st on LH needle tbl, then knit 2nd st on LH needle tbl, then knit 1st st on LH needle; sl all 3 sts from needle.

Right Mitt

CO 32 (36) sts. Divide evenly between 4 dpns and join to work in the rnd.

Cuff

Work 8 rnds in Twisted Rib.

Arm

Setup rnd: Work Row 2 of Seed St over 13 (15) sts, pfb, k3, pfb, k3, pfb, work Row 2 of Seed St over rem 10 (12) sts—35 (39) sts.

Rnd 1: Work Row 1 of Seed St over 13 (15) sts, p2, work Row 1 of Twisted Panel Right over 3 sts, p2, work Row 1 of Twisted Panel Left over 3 sts, p2, work Row 1 of Seed St to end.

Rnd 2: Work Row 2 of Seed St over 13 (15 sts), p2, work Row 2 of Twisted Panel Right over 3 sts, p2, work Row 2 of Twisted Panel Left over 3 sts, p2, work Row 2 of Seed St to end.

Rnd 3: Work Row 1 of Seed St over 13 (15 sts), p2, work Row 3 of Twisted Panel Right over 3 sts, p2, work Row 3 of Twisted Panel Left over 3 sts, p2, work Row 1 of Seed St to end.

Rnd 4: Work Row 2 of Seed St over 13 (15 sts), p2, work Row 4 of Twisted Panel Right over 3 sts, p2, work Row 4 of Twisted Panel Left over 3 sts, p2, work Row 2 of Seed St to end.

Rep Rnds 1-4 two more times.

Thumb Gusset

Rnd 1 (inc): Work in patt over 13 (15) sts, p2, k3, p1, pm, m1P, pm, p1, k3, p2, work in patt to end—1 st inc'd.

Rnd 2: Work in patt to m, p2, work in patt to end.

Rnd 3 (inc): Work in patt to m, m1P, purl to m, m1P, work in patt to end—2 sts inc'd.

Rnd 4: Work in patt to m, purl to m, work in patt to end.

Rep last 2 rnds 5 (6) more times—13 (15) Thumb sts.

Hand

Next rnd: Work to m, remove m, slip Thumb sts onto waste yarn, remove m, work to end—35 (39) sts rem.

Work in patt for 13 (15) rnds.

Next rnd: Work Row 2 of Seed St over 13 (15) sts, k1 tbl, [p2tog, k1tbl, p1, k1tbl] twice, p2tog, work in Seed St to end—32 (36) sts rem.

Work in Twisted Rib for 3 rnds. Knit 2 rnds. BO all sts loosely.

Thumb

Divide held Thumb sts evenly between 3 dpns. Beg at center of Thumb gap, pick up and purl 2 sts, p13 (15), pick up and purl 1—16 (18) sts.

Dec rnd: P1, p2tog, purl to last 2 sts, p2tog—14 (16) sts rem.

Purl 1 rnd. Knit 1 rnd. BO all sts loosely.

Left Mitt

Work as for Right Mitt.

Finishing

Weave in loose ends.

TIP ✷ Keeping track of where you are in Seed Stitch pattern is a snap! Always knit into a purl stitch (the stitch that looks like a bump), and purl into a knit stitch (the stitch that looks like a "v").

Energy
Mitts

50

The smooth, flowing lines in Energy Mitts are the result of shaped intarsia. Increases and decreases are worked in the gray sections only, while the stitch counts for the yellow and black stripes remain consistent. Working intarsia with four colors may seem daunting, but this small project is the perfect place to give it a try. Smooth worsted weight yarn makes the stitches big enough to see and relatively easy to manage.

FINISHED MEASUREMENTS
Hand circumference: 7½"/19 cm
Length: 6½"/16.5 cm

YARN
Deborah Norville Collection Everyday Soft Worsted by Premier Yarns, medium worsted weight #4 yarn (100% anti-pilling acrylic; 203 yd/4 oz, 186 m/113 g per skein)
• 1 skein #100-12 Black (MC)
• 1 skein #100-24 Steel (CC1)
• 1 skein #100-23 Mist (CC2)
• 1 skein #100-37 Fluorescent Yellow (CC3)

NEEDLES AND OTHER MATERIALS
• US 7 (4.5 mm) set of 5 double-pointed needles (dpns)
• Two 7"/18 cm closed-bottom metal zippers
• Stitch marker
• Tapestry needle
• Sewing needle and thread

GAUGE
18 sts x 24 rows in St st = 4"/10 cm square
Be sure to check your gauge!

NOTES
• The hand of this mitt is worked sideways. Stitches are picked up along the sides of the mitt after the main piece is finished for the top and bottom ribbing.
• When changing colors in the hand section, use the intarsia method (see page 110 for a tutorial).
• When working a make 1 (m1) increase, be sure to insert your needle into the strand between the next 2 stitches that is the *same* color as the stitch you are increasing.
• The thumbhole is formed in an unusual way. When working Rows 19–24, and where indicated by the red line, do not twist the yarn when changing colors. Add a second strand of MC at the red line to work sts on the other side of the thumbhole. This will form a hole.

Right Mitt

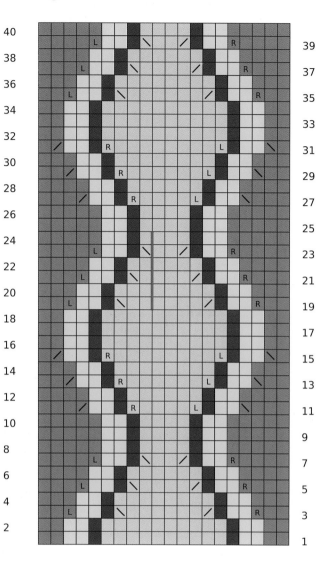

Left Mitt

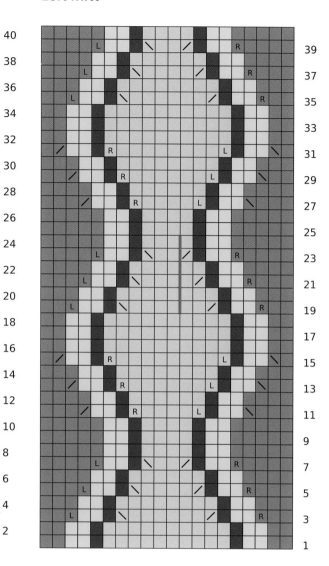

Key

☐ knit on RS, purl on WS

■ MC

▨ CC1

▨ CC2

▢ CC3

◪ k2tog

◩ ssk

R m1R

L m1L

┃ do not twist yarn

Right Mitt

Placket

With CC1, CO 20 sts to 1 dpn; do not join. Purl 1 row. Knit 2 rows.

Hand

Knit 1 row. Purl 1 row.

Work Rows 1-38 of Right Mitt chart, changing colors as indicated. Break all colors except CC1.

With CC1, knit 1 row. Purl 1 row.

Placket

Knit 3 rows. Bind off all sts pwise

Top Edging

With MC and with RS facing you, pick up and knit 34 sts evenly along edge, skipping 3 rows of Placket at each end. Divide sts evenly among 4 dpn. Pm and join to work in the rnd.

Rnd 1: CO 2 sts using backward lp method, * k1, p1; rep from * to end—36 sts.

Rnd 2: * K1, p1; rep from * to end.

Rnds 3–4: Rep Rnd 2. BO all sts loosely in patt.

Cuff

With MC and with RS facing you, pick up and knit 3 sts along Placket on bottom edge of mitt, 33 sts evenly along Hand, and 3 sts along other Placket edge—39 sts. Do not join.

Row 1 (WS): P2, * k1, p1; rep from * to last 3 sts, k1, p2.

Row 2 (RS): K2, * p1, k1; rep from * to last 3 sts, p1, k2.

Rows 3–8: Rep Rows 1 & 2. BO all sts loosely in patt.

Left Mitt

Work as for Right Mitt, following Left Mitt chart.

Finishing

Weave in ends. Lightly steam block mitt.

Fold under zipper tape on each side at the open end. Tack into place with sewing needle and thread. Pin one side of zipper to Placket, right sides tog. Sew zipper to Placket using short, even stitches and backstitching every inch. Rep for other side of zipper and Placket. Invisibly whipstitch edges of zipper tape to inside of mitt.

Sprout
Mitts

Sprout Mitts are the perfect little thing to slip on your hands on a sunny April day. The cotton/silk blend will provide your hands with relief from the spring chill without making them too warm. After these mitts are knit, clear elastic is sewn into the cuff, allowing you to adjust your own pair for a perfect fit.

FINISHED MEASUREMENTS
Hand circumference: 6¼ (7)"/16 (18) cm unstretched;
   8 (9)"/20.5 (23) cm stretched
Length: 8¾ (9)"/22 (23) cm

YARN
Deborah Norville Collection Cotton Soft Silk by Premier Yarns, medium worsted #4 yarn (78% cotton, 22% silk; 152 yd/3 oz, 139 m/85 g per skein)
• 1 skein #950-07 Lime

NEEDLES AND OTHER MATERIALS
• US 6 (4 mm) set of 5 double-pointed needles (dpns)
• Tapestry needle
• Stitch markers
• Waste yarn
• Two 12"/30.5 cm lengths ⅛"/.5 cm clear elastic

GAUGE
18 sts x 26 rows in St st = 4"/10 cm square
Be sure to check your gauge!

Right Mitt

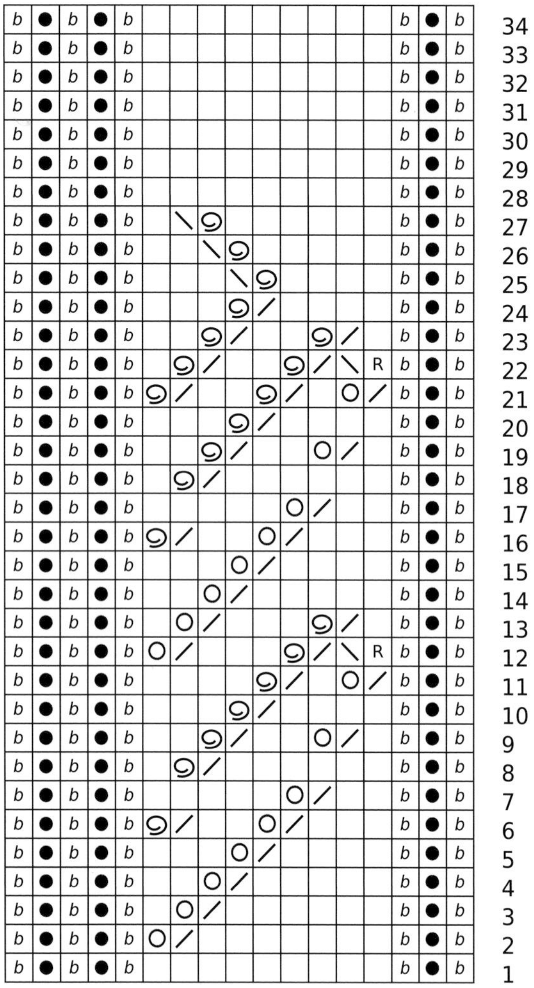

Left Mitt

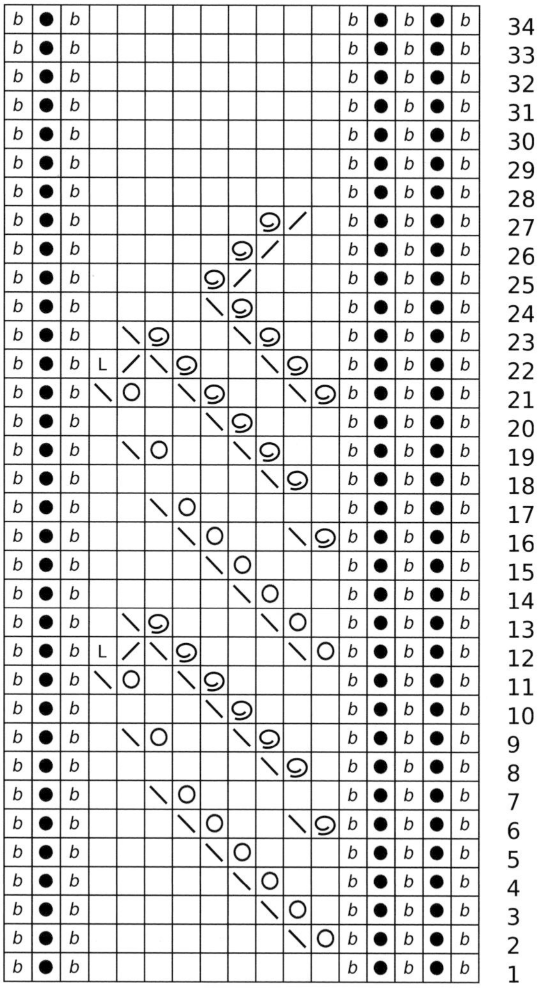

Key

- knit
- yo
- k2tog
- ssk
- purl
- L m1L
- R m1R
- b k1 tbl
- CO 1 st using backward lp CO

Right Mitt

CO 96 (108) sts. Divide evenly between 4 dpns and join to work in the rnd.

Cuff

Dec rnd: * BO 2 sts pwise, p1; rep from * to end—32 (36) sts rem.

Purl 1 rnd. Knit 1 rnd.

Inc rnd: Purl to last st, pfb—33 (37) sts.

Hand

Rnd 1: K0 (1), work Row 1 of Right Mitt chart over 16 sts, knit to end.

Rnd 2: K0 (1), work next row of Right Mitt chart over 16 sts, knit to end.

Rep last rnd 3 more times.

Thumb Gusset

Inc rnd: Work in patt across 18 (20) sts, pm, yo, pm, knit to end—1 st inc'd.

Next rnd: Work in patt to m, knit to end.

Inc rnd: Work in patt to m, yo, knit to m, yo, knit to end—2 sts inc'd.

Next rnd: Work in patt to m, knit to end.

Rep last 2 rnds 4 (5) more times—11 (13) Thumb sts.

Next rnd: Work in patt to m, sl Thumb sts to waste yarn, knit to end—33 (37) sts rem.

Cont in patt through Row 30 (34) of Right Mitt chart.

[Purl 1 rnd, knit 1 rnd.] twice. BO all sts pwise.

Thumb

Place 11 (13) held Thumb sts evenly onto 3 dpns. Beg at center of Thumb gap, pick up and knit 2 sts, k11 (13), pick up and knit 1—14 (16) sts.

Dec rnd: K1, k2tog, knit to last 3 sts, ssk, k1—12 (14) sts rem.

Knit 2 rnds. BO all sts loosely pwise.

Left Mitt

CO 96 (108) sts. Divide evenly between 4 dpns and join to work in the rnd.

Cuff

Work as for Right Mitt.

Hand

Rnd 1: K0 (1), work Row 1 of Left Mitt chart over 16 sts, knit to end.

Rnd 2: K0 (1), work next row of Left Mitt chart over 16 sts, knit to end.

Rep last rnd 3 more times.

Thumb Gusset

Inc rnd: Work in patt to last 2 sts, pm, yo, pm, knit to end—1 st inc'd.

Next rnd: Work in patt to m, knit to end.

Inc rnd: Work in patt to m, yo, knit to m, yo, knit to end—2 sts inc'd.

Next rnd: Work in patt to m, knit to end.

Rep last 2 rnds 4 (5) more times—11 (13) Thumb sts.

Next rnd: Work in patt to m, sl Thumb sts to waste yarn, knit to end—33 (37) sts rem.

Cont in patt through row 30 (34) of Left Mitt chart.

[Purl 1 rnd, knit 1 rnd.] twice. BO all sts pwise

Thumb

Work as for Right Mitt.

Finishing

Weave in loose ends. Thread elastic through tapestry needle. With WS facing, weave elastic through back side of Rnd 1 of Hand. Tighten elastic to about 6 (7)"/15 (17.5) cm, tie ends securely in knot. Weave in ends of elastic; trim.

Little Bow

ntimidated by felting but always wanted to give it a try? Then these mitts are for you! Only two small parts of each mitt are felted, the cuff and bow. After the felting process is complete and these pieces are dry, the rest of the mitt is knit. Although it may look like stranded knitting, the checked pattern is worked using only one color at a time, slipping stitches to create the checked colorwork effect.

FINISHED MEASUREMENTS

Hand circumference: 7½ (9¼)"/19 (23.5) cm
Length: 6½ (7½)"/16.5 (19) cm

YARN

Premier Yarns Wool Worsted, medium worsted weight #4 yarn (100% wool; 186 yd/3.5 oz, 170 m/ 100 g per skein)
• 1 skein #35-120 Raspberry (A)
• 1 skein #35-121 Charcoal (B)
• 1 skein #35-101 Cream (C)

NEEDLES AND OTHER MATERIALS

• US 8 (5 mm) straight needles
• US 6 (4 mm) set of 5 double-pointed needles (dpns)
• 2 spare US 6 (4 mm) or smaller dpns
• Tapestry needle
• Stitch markers
• Worsted weight cotton or other nonfelting waste yarn
• Two ¼"/.5 cm pearl beads
• Sewing needle and thread
• US G-6 (4 mm) crochet hook

GAUGE

Using larger needles,16 sts x 28 rows in Garter st BEFORE
    felting = 4"/10 cm square
Using larger needles, 18 sts x 32 rows in Garter st AFTER
    felting = 4"/10 cm square
Using smaller needles, 20 sts x 44 rows = 4"/10 cm in
    Checks patt
Be sure to check your gauge!

STITCH GUIDE

Checks Pattern (multiple of 4 sts + 2)

Rnd 1: With A, knit.

Rnds 2 & 3: With B, * sl 1, k2, [sl 2, k2] 4 (5) times, k2; rep from * once more.

Rnd 4: With A, knit.

Rnd 5: With C, * sl 3, [k2, sl 2] 4 (5) times; rep from * once more.

Rep Rnds 1–6 for patt.

Checks Pattern

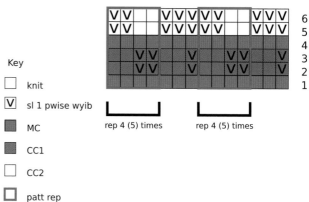

Key

☐ knit

Ⓥ sl 1 pwise wyib

▨ MC

▨ CC1

☐ CC2

☐ patt rep

rep 4 (5) times   rep 4 (5) times

Felted Cuff (make 2)

With larger needles and A, CO 32 (38) sts.

Row 1: Knit.

Row 2: K1, m1L, knit to end—33 (39) sts.

Row 3: Knit to last st, m1L, k1—34 (40) sts.

Row 4: K1, m1L, knit to end—35 (41) sts.

Row 5: Knit.

Row 6: K1, k2tog, knit to end—34 (40) sts rem.

Row 7: Knit to last 3 sts, ssk, k1—33 (39) sts rem.

Row 8: K1, k2tog, pass first st knit over k2tog st (1 st rem on RH needle), BO 3 more sts, sl rem 28 (34) sts onto waste yarn. Secure ends of waste yarn. Secure end of working yarn. Clip ends to 3".

Bow (make 2)

With larger needles and A, CO 7 sts.

Rows 1–6: Knit.

Row 7: K1, k2tog, k1, ssk, k1—5 sts rem.

Row 8: Knit.

Row 9: K1, sl 1, k2tog, psso, k1—3 sts rem.

Rows 10-14: Knit.

Row 15: K1, m1L, k1, m1L, k1—5 sts.

Row 16: Knit.

Row 17: K1, m1L, k3, m1L, k1—7 sts.

Rows 18–23: Knit.

BO all sts.

With B and crochet hook, sl st evenly around perimeter of Bow, working 6 sl st along short ends of Bow and 1 sl st in every other row along sides, taking care not to work sts too tightly. Fasten off. Clip ends to 3"/7.5 cm and weave in.

Felting

Place Cuffs and Bows into lingerie bag or pillowcase. Tie bag or pillowcase closed, so pieces cannot escape during felting process. Place bag in washing machine with a couple of towels or articles of clothing. Run washing machine through normal cycle using warm water. Check items for felting progress. If not felted to listed measurements, continue agitating 5 minutes at a time until correct size is achieved. The cuffs should be 7¾ (9)"/19.5 (23) cm wide at their widest point, and the bow should be 2"/5 cm wide. Pat items into shape, lay flat to dry. Before Cuffs are fully dry, carefully insert spare dpn into held sts and remove waste yarn.

Cuffs should be fully dry before proceeding to Arm.

Right Arm

Lay out Cuff in front of you so shaped end is on the right, and held sts are on the far side, away from you. Join A where you left off, at the right-hand side of the piece.

Smaller Size Only
Rnd 1: With smaller dpns, * [k4, m1L] 2 times, [k3, m1L] 2 times; rep from * once—38 sts.

Larger Size Only
Rnd 1: With A, * [k3, m1L] 5 times, k2, m1L; rep from * once more—46 sts.

Both Sizes
Divide sts evenly between 4 dpns and join to work in the rnd. K10 (12), pm; this is now beg of rnd.
Work Rnds 1-6 of Checks patt 6 (7) times.

Thumb Opening
Next rnd: Work Rnd 1 of Checks patt over 3 sts, k6 with waste yarn, sl these 6 sts back to RH needle, knit across these 6 sts, knit to end.

Hand
Work Rnds 2–6 of Checks patt once, rep Rnds 1–6 of patt once (twice), then rep Rnds 1 and 2 of patt once. Break B and C.
Next rnd: With A, * k1, [sl 2, k2] 4 (5) times, sl 2; rep from * once more.
Knit 1 rnd. Purl 1 rnd. Knit 2 rnds. Purl 1 rnd. BO all sts pwise.

Thumb
Hold 2 spare dpns parallel, With a third dpn, carefully remove waste yarn, 1 st at a time. Place upper 6 sts on one dpn, and lower 6 sts on the other.
Rnd 1: With A, pick up and knit 2 sts from side of Thumb gap, k6 sts from needle, pick up and knit 2 sts from other side of Thumb gap, k6 from other needle—16 sts.
Dec rnd: * K2tog, k6; rep from * once more—14 sts rem.
Knit 2 rnds. BO all sts pwise.

Left Arm

Lay out Cuff in front of you so shaped end is on the left, and held sts are on the far side, away from you. Join A at the right-hand side of the piece.

Smaller Size Only
Rnd 1: With smaller dpns, * [k4, m1L] 2 times, [k3, m1L] 2 times; rep from * once—38 sts.

Larger Size Only
Rnd 1: With A, * [k3, kfb] 5 times, k2, kfb; rep from * once more—46 sts.

Both Sizes
Divide sts evenly between 4 dpns and join to work in the rnd. K10 (12), pm; this is now beg of rnd.
Work Rnds 1–6 of Checks patt 6 (7) times.

Thumb Opening
Next rnd: Work Rnd 1 of Checks patt over 11 (15) sts, k6 with waste yarn, sl these 6 sts back to RH needle, knit across these 6 sts, knit to end.

Hand
Work Rnds 2–6 of Checks patt once, rep Rnds 1–6 of patt once (twice), then rep Rnds 1 and 2 of patt once. Break B and C.
Next rnd: With A, * k1, [sl 2, k2] 4 (5) times, sl 2; rep from * once more.
Knit 1 rnd. Purl 1 rnd. Knit 2 rnds. Purl 1 rnd. BO all sts, pwise.

Thumb
Hold 2 spare dpns parallel. With a third dpn, carefully remove waste yarn, 1 st at a time. Place upper 6 sts on one dpn, and lower 6 sts on the other.
Rnd 1: With A, pick up and knit 2 sts from side of Thumb gap, k6 sts from needle, pick up and knit 2 sts from other side of Thumb gap, k6 from other needle—16 sts.
Dec rnd: * K2tog, k6; rep from * once more—14 sts rem.
Knit 2 rnds. BO all sts pwise.

Finishing

Weave in ends. Sew a bead to top of each Bow. Sew Bow to top of mitt, centered on top of Hand, with center of Bow 1"/ 2.54 cm from top edge. Sew female part of snap to Cuff tab. Sew male part of snap to Cuff, directly beneath tab.

Fade Fingerless Gloves

I love linen stitch in knitting. It's a simple two-row, two-stitch repeat that resembles woven fabric. These linen-stitch gloves take advantage of the slipped stitches while transitioning from one color to the next. Try three shades in the same range of hues for a smooth color change, or use three highly contrasting tones for a starker effect.

FINISHED MEASUREMENTS
Hand circumference: 7 (8¼)"/18 (21) cm
Length: 8½ (9)"/21.5 (23) cm

YARN
Premier Yarns Cotton Fair, fine weight #2 yarn (52% cotton, 48% acrylic; 317 yd/3.5 oz, 290 m/100 g)
• 1 skein #2702 Cream (A)
• 1 skein #2703 Baby Blue (B)
• 1 skein #2710 Leaf Green (C)

NEEDLES AND OTHER MATERIALS
• US 3 (3.25 mm) set of 5 double-pointed needles (dpns)
• US 4 (3.5 mm) set of 5 dpns
• 4 spare US 3 (3.25 mm) or smaller dpns
• Tapestry needle
• Stitch markers
• Waste yarn

GAUGE
Using larger needles, 28 sts x 42 rows in Linen Stitch =
    4"/10 cm square
Be sure to check your gauge!

NOTES
• When changing colors at the beginning of a round, bring the new color up and around the previous color; this will prevent holes from forming.

STITCH GUIDE
Linen Stitch (Linen St) (odd number of sts)
   Rnd 1: * K1, sl 1 pwise wyif; rep from * to last st, k1.
   Rnd 2: * Sl 1 pwise wyif, k1; rep from * to last st, sl 1.
   Rep Rnds 1 & 2 for patt.

Stripes

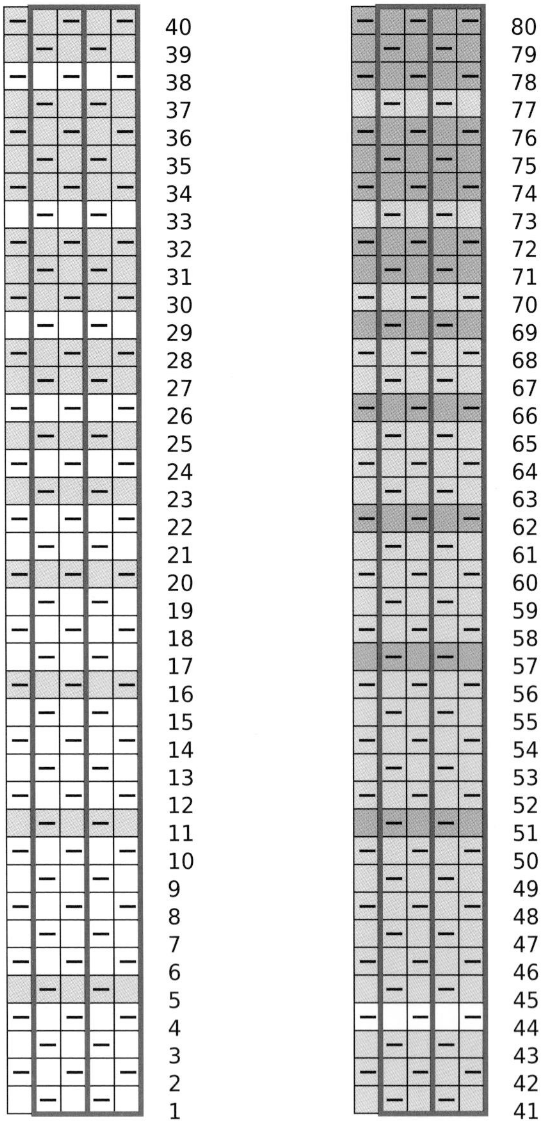

				40
				39
				38

(Stripes chart, left column rows 1–40, right column rows 41–80)

Key

- ☐ knit
- ☐ A
- ☐ B
- ☐ C
- ⊟ sl 1 wyif
- ☐ patt rep

Right Glove

Thumb

With smaller dpn needles and A, CO 20 (22) sts. Divide evenly between 3 dpns and join to work in the rnd. Knit 6 (8) rnds. Sl first 10 (11) sts onto spare dpn and last 10 (11) sts onto second dpn. Break yarn.

Pinky Finger

With smaller dpn needles and A, CO 14 (16) sts. Divide evenly between 3 dpns and join to work in the rnd. Knit 6 (8) rnds. Sl first 7 (8) sts onto a spare dpn and last 7 (8) sts onto a second spare dpn. Break yarn.

Ring Finger

With smaller dpn needles and A, CO 16 (18) sts. Divide evenly between 3 dpns and join to work in the rnd. Knit 6 (8) rnds. Sl first 8 (9) sts onto first spare dpn next to first 7 (8) Pinky sts, and last 8 (9) sts onto second dpn next to last 7 (8) Pinky sts. Break yarn.

Middle Finger

Work as for Ring Finger. Sl first 8 (9) sts onto first spare dpn next to first 8 (9) Ring Finger sts, and last 8 (9) sts onto second dpn next to last 8 (9) Ring Finger sts. Break yarn.

Index Finger

With smaller dp n needles and A, CO 15 (17) sts. Divide evenly between 3 dpns and join to work in the rnd. Knit 5 (7) rnds.

Join Fingers

Next rnd: Knit to last 2 sts of Index Finger, ssk; working across first Middle Finger sts, k2tog, k4 (5), ssk; working across first Ring Finger sts, k2tog, k4 (5), ssk; working across Pinky, ssk, k10 (12), k2tog; working across rem Ring Finger sts, k2tog, k4 (5), ssk; working across rem Middle Finger sts, k2tog, k4 (5), ssk; working across rem Index Finger sts, k2tog, k19 (22), pm for beg of rnd—49 (57) sts.

Hand

Knit 1 rnd. Switch to larger needles.

Larger Size Only

With A, work Rnds 1 and 2 of Linen St twice.

Both Sizes

Work Rows 1–15 of Stripes chart.

Thumb Gusset

Next rnd: Work Row 16 of Stripes chart to last 11 (13) sts, pm, sl 1, sl this st to LH Thumb needle, ssk, work in patt to last Thumb st, sl 1, sl this st to LH Glove needle, k2tog, pm, work in patt to end—2 sts dec'd, 67 (77) sts rem.

Next 2 rnds: Work Rows 17 & 18 of Stripes chart to end.

Dec rnd: Work next row of Stripes chart to m, ssk, work in patt to 2 sts before m, k2tog, work in patt to end—2 sts dec'd.

Work Rows 20–40 of Stripes chart, working Dec rnd on Rows 22, 25, 28, 31, 33, 35, 37, 39—49 (59) sts rem.

Larger Size Only

Rep Dec rnd on Row 41 of chart—57 sts rem.

Both Sizes

Cont in patt through Row 80 of chart.

Larger Size Only

With C, work 4 rnds in Linen St.

Cuff

Switch to smaller needles.

Dec rnd: With C, * K2tog, k4 (5); rep from * to last 7 (8) sts, k2tog, k3 (4), k2tog—40 (48) sts rem.

Next rnd: * K1, p1; rep from * to end. Rep this rnd 5 more times. Knit 3 rnds. BO all sts.

Left Glove

Work as for Right Glove to Thumb Gusset.

Thumb Gusset

Next rnd: Work Row 16 of Stripes chart across 11 (13) sts, pm, sl 1, sl this st to LH Thumb needle, ssk, work in patt to last Thumb st, sl 1, sl this st to LH Glove needle, k2tog, pm, work in patt to end—2 sts dec'd, 67 (77) sts rem.

Comp as for Right Glove.

Finishing

Using yarn ends, sew up holes between fingers. Sew Thumb gap closed. Weave in loose ends. Wet block to even out knitting.

It's a Plaid
Plaid World

I t's punk rock, it's preppy, it's lumberjack; plaid is so many things to so many genres. Make these your own by choosing colors that let the world know just what kind of plaid person you are. The plaid hand portion of the pattern is worked back and forth in rows. The buttonhole and button bands are worked sideways by picking up stitches from the sides of the hand.

FINISHED MEASUREMENTS

Hand circumference: 8 (9)"/20.5 (23) cm unbuttoned;
 7½ (8½)"/19 (21.5) cm buttoned
Length: 5¾"/14.5 cm

YARN

Deborah Norville Collection Serenity Sock Solids by Premier Yarns, superfine weight #1 yarn (50% superwash merino, 25% rayon from bamboo, 25% nylon; 230 yd/1.75 oz, 210 m/50 g per skein)
• 1 skein #06 Deep Brown (A)
• 1 skein #02 Hot Pink (B)
• 1 skein #05 Burgundy (C)
• 1 skein #03 Red (D)

NEEDLES AND OTHER MATERIALS

• Two 8"/20.5 cm US 1 (2.25 mm) double-pointed needles (dpns) or one 24"/61 cm (or longer) circular needle
• Tapestry needle
• US B-1 (2.25 mm) crochet hook
• Seven ⁷⁄₁₆"/1 cm buttons

GAUGE

36 sts x 38 rows in Plaid patt = 4"/10 cm square
40 sts x 44 rows in K1, P1 ribbing = 4"/10 cm square
 Be sure to check your gauge!

Plaid Pattern

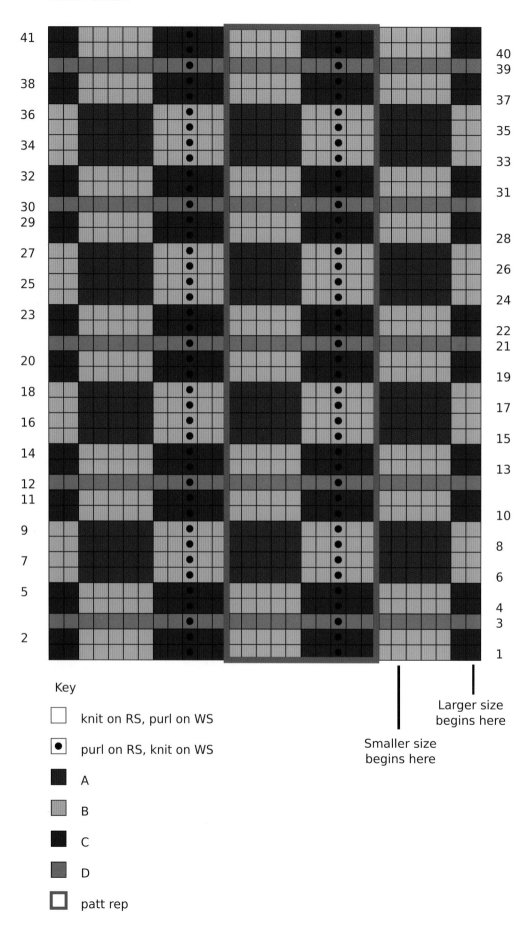

Key

☐ knit on RS, purl on WS

⊡ purl on RS, knit on WS

■ A

▦ B

■ C

▮ D

☐ patt rep

NOTES

- When working Row 3 of Plaid patt, knit across sts from the RS with D. Slide sts back to other end of needle and continue in pattern. Row 12, the next D row, will be a WS (purl) row, and so on.
- It's important to block the mitts before adding the Button and Buttonhole Bands.
- When picking up sts for Button Band and Buttonhole Band, work 2 sts in from each edge.
- The rev St st columns in the Plaid patt indicate where the applied crochet lines are to be worked.

STITCH GUIDE

K1, P1 Ribbing (odd number of sts)
Row 1 (RS): * K1, p1; rep from * to last st, k1.
Row 2 (WS): * P1, k1; rep from * to last st, p1.
Rep Rows 1 & 2 for patt.

1-Row Buttonhole
Bring yarn to front, sl next st pwise, take yarn to back, sl next st, pass first slipped st over last slipped st (1 st bound off), * sl next st, pass first slipped st over last slipped st (1 st bound off); rep from * 12 (16) more times—13 (17) sts bound off.

Sl last bound-off st on RH needle to LH needle. Turn, using knitted cast on, cast on 14 (18) sts to last st on RH needle, sl last cast-on st to LH needle, pass 2nd st on LH needle over last cast-on st, sl cast-on st back to LH needle, turn, cont in patt.

Applied Chained Crochet Lines
Holding the yarn beneath the fabric, insert crochet hook from the front through the center of the first knit stitch. Yo and pull through the stitch to the front—1 loop on hook.

* Insert hook from the front through the center of the next stitch. Yo and pull up a loop through the stitch—2 loops on hook.

Pull the second yo through the first—1 loop rem on hook.

Repeat from * until all stitches have been worked. Cut yarn and pull the end through the loop to secure it, then pull it through to the back of the work to weave it in.

(See page 118 for full step-by-step instructions with photos.)

Right Mitt

With A, CO 49 (59) sts.

Cuff
Beg with RS row, work 9 rows of K1, P1 Ribbing.
Inc row (WS): P7, m1p, [p4 (5), m1p] 9 times, purl to end—59 (69) sts

Hand
Work Rows 1–20 of Plaid patt.

Thumb
Next row: Work Row 21 of patt across 17 (21) sts, work 1-Row Buttonhole over 13 (17) sts, work in patt to end.
Cont in patt through Row 41. Break all colors except A.

Top Edging
With A, knit 1 row. Work 5 rows of K1, P1 Ribbing. BO all sts loosely in patt.
Block Mitt.

Buttonhole Band
With RS facing and A, beg at lower RH cuff, pick up and knit 61 sts evenly along entire RH side of Mitt, about 1 st for every row.
Row 1 (WS): Work Row 2 of K1, P1 Ribbing.
Rows 2–5: Cont in K1, P1 Ribbing.
Row 6 (RS): [K1, p1] twice, k1, * yo twice, [p1, k1] 5 times; rep from * 4 more times, yo twice, [p1, k1] 3 times—6 Buttonholes.
Row 7: [P1, k1] twice, p1, * k2tog, p2tog tbl, [k1, p1] 4 times; rep from * 4 more times, k2tog, p2tog tbl, [k1, p1] twice.
Rows 8–10: Work in K1, P1 Ribbing.
BO all sts in patt.

Button Band
With RS facing and A, beg at upper LH Top Edge, pick up and knit 61 sts evenly along entire LH side of Mitt, approx 1 st for every row.
Beg with WS row, work 12 rows in K1, P1 ribbing. BO all sts in patt.
Weave in loose ends.

Left Mitt

Work as for Right Mitt through Row 20 of Plaid patt.

Thumb

Next row: Work Row 21 of patt across 28 (31) sts, work
   1-Row Buttonhole over 13 (17) sts, work in patt to end.
Comp Hand and Top Edging as for Right Mitt.

Buttonhole Band

With RS facing and A, beg at upper LH Top Edge, pick up
and knit 61 sts evenly along entire LH side of Mitt. Comp
as for Right Buttonhole Band.

Button Band

Working along other side of Mitt, pick up sts and comp
Button Band as for Right Mitt.

Finishing

Using D and crochet hook, beg in Row 1 of first rev St st
column, work Applied Chained Crochet Line up entire
length of rev St st column. Repeat for other rev St st
columns.

Thumb Edging

With crochet hook and A, attach yarn at edge of Thumb-
   hole. Chain 1, single crochet in same space, single crochet in each st around, join with sl st to beg single
   crochet. Fasten off.
Sew buttons to Button Band opposite Buttonholes.

Troubled Water

ideways cuff construction, cables, and a unique thumb opening await you in this fun gauntlet-length mitt pattern. The cuff is knit and seamed, then stitches are picked up along the side of the cuff, and the arm of the mitt is knit upward. The arm and hand are worked in the round up to the thumb, then back and forth in rows to create an opening for the thumb. A strategically placed cable cross makes the thumb opening look smooth and seamless.

FINISHED MEASUREMENTS
Hand circumference: 6 (7½)"/15 (19) cm unstretched; 8
    (9¾)"/20.5 (25) cm stretched
    Length: 9"/23 cm

YARN
Premier Yarns Wool Worsted, medium worsted #4 yarn
(100% wool; 186 yd/3.5 oz, 170 m/100 g per skein)
• 1 skein #35-119 Mermaid

NEEDLES AND OTHER MATERIALS
• US 7 (4.5 mm) set of 5 double-pointed needles (dpns)
• 2 cable needles
• Tapestry needle
• Waste yarn

GAUGE
16 sts x 22 rows in St st = 4"/10 cm square
Be sure to check your gauge!

NOTES
• Slip stitches purlwise with yarn in front.

STITCH GUIDE
3x3 Left Cross (3x3 LC)
Slip next 3 sts to cn and hold in front, k3 from LH needle,
k3 from cn.

3x3 Right Cross (3x3 RC)
Slip next 3 sts to cn and hold in back, k3 from LH needle,
k3 from cn.

3x2x3 Left Cross (3x2x3 LC)
Slip next 3 sts to cn and hold in front, slip next 2 sts to cn
and hold in back, k3 from LH needle, p2 from back cn, k3
from front cn.

3x2x3 Right Cross (3x2x3 RC)
Slip next 5 sts to cn and hold in back, k3 from LH needle,
slip 2 sts from left end of cn to LH needle, p2, k3 from cn.

Right Mitt
Cuff
CO 15 sts.
Row 1 (RS): Sl 2, k6, p1, k5, p1.
Row 2: K7, p6, k2.
Row 3: Sl 2, 3x3 RC, p1, k5, p1.
Row 4: K1, p5, k1, p6, k2.
Row 5: Rep Row 1.
Row 6: Rep Row 2.
Rep these 6 rows 7 (9) more times.
BO all sts in patt. Sew BO edge to CO edge.

Arm

With seam facing, beg at noncabled edge of Cuff, at top of garter ridge just to the right of seam, * pick up and knit 1 st, pick up and knit 1 st from side of next row, pick up and knit 1 st at top of next garter ridge, pick up and knit 2 sts along side of St st section; rep from * 7 (9) more times—40 (50) sts. Divide sts evenly between 4 dpns.

Rnd 1: * K3, p2; rep from * to end.

Rnds 2–7: Rep Rnd 1.

Rnd 8: * 3x2x3 RC, p2; rep from * to end.

Rnds 9–14: Rep Rnd 1.

Rnd 15: * K3, p2; rep from * 6 (8) more times. This is new beg of rnd.

Rnd 16: * 3x2x3 LC, p2; rep from * to end.

Thumb

Rnd 1 (WS): * K3, p2; rep from * to end.

Note: Remainder of Thumb section is worked back in forth in rows.

Row 2 (RS): * K3, p2; rep from * to end, k3, p1, turn.

Row 3 (WS): K1, * p3, k2; rep from * to last 4 sts, p3, k1.

Row 4: P1, * k3, p2; rep from * to last 4 sts, k3, p1.

Row 5: Rep Row 3.

Row 6: Rep Row 4.

Row 7: Rep Row 3.

Row 8: P1, * 3x2x3 RC, p2; rep from * to last 9 sts, 3x2x3 RC, p1.

Row 9: Rep Row 3.

Row 10: Rep Row 4.

Row 11: Rep Row 3.

Row 12: Rep Row 4; do not turn.

Hand

Rejoin to work in the rnd.

Rnd 1: P1, * k3, p2; rep from * to last 4 sts. This is new beg of rnd.

Rnds 2 & 3: * K3, p2; rep from * to end.

Rnd 4: * 3x2x3 LC, p2; rep from * to end.

Rnds 5–8: * K3, p2; rep from * to end.

Rnd 9: * P3, p2tog; rep from * to end—32 (36) sts rem.

Rnd 10: Knit.

BO all sts pwise.

Left Mitt

Cuff

CO 15 sts.

Row 1 (RS): Sl 2, k6, p1, k5, p1.

Row 2: K7, p6, k2.

Row 3: Sl 2, 3x3 LC, p1, k5, p1.

Row 4: K1, p5, k1, p6, k2.

Row 5: Rep Row 1.

Row 6: Rep Row 2.

Rep these 6 rows 7 (9) more times.

BO all sts in patt.

Arm

With seam facing, beg at noncabled edge of Cuff, at top of garter ridge just to the right of seam, * pick up and knit 1 st, pick up and knit 1 st from side of next row, pick up and knit 1 st at top of next garter ridge, pick up and knit 2 sts along side of St st section; rep from * 7 (9) more times—40 (50) sts. Divide sts evenly between 4 dpns.

Rnd 1: * K3, p2; rep from * to end.

Rnds 2–7: Rep Rnd 1.

Rnd 8: * 3x2x3 LC, p2; rep from * to end.

Rnds 9–14: Rep Rnd 1.

Rnd 15: K3, p2; this is new beg of rnd.

Rnd 16: * 3x2x3 RC, p2; rep from * to end.

Thumb

Rnd 1 (WS): * K3, p2; rep from * to end.

Note: Remainder of Thumb section is worked back in forth in rows.

Row 2 (RS): * K3, p2; rep from * to last 10 sts, k3, p1, turn.

Row 3 (WS): K1, * p3, k2; rep from * to last 4 sts, p3, k1.

Row 4: P1, * k3, p2; rep from * to last 4 sts, k3, p1.

Row 5: Rep Row 3.

Row 6: Rep Row 4.

Row 7: Rep Row 3.

Row 8: P1, * 3x2x3 LC, p2; rep from * to last 9 sts, 3x2x3 LC, p1.

Row 9: Rep Row 3.

Row 10: Rep Row 4.

Row 11: Rep Row 3.

Row 12: Rep Row 4; do not turn.

Hand

Rejoin to work in the rnd.

Rnd 1: P1, * k3, p2; rep from * to last 4 sts. This is new beg of rnd.

Rnds 2 & 3: * K3, p2; rep from * to end.

Rnd 4: * 3x2x3 RC, p2; rep from * to end.

Rnds 5–8: * K3, p2; rep from * to end.

Rnd 9: * P3, p2tog; rep from * to end—32 (36) sts rem.

Rnd 10: Knit.

BO all sts, pwise.

Finishing

Weave in loose ends.

Slouchy Mitts

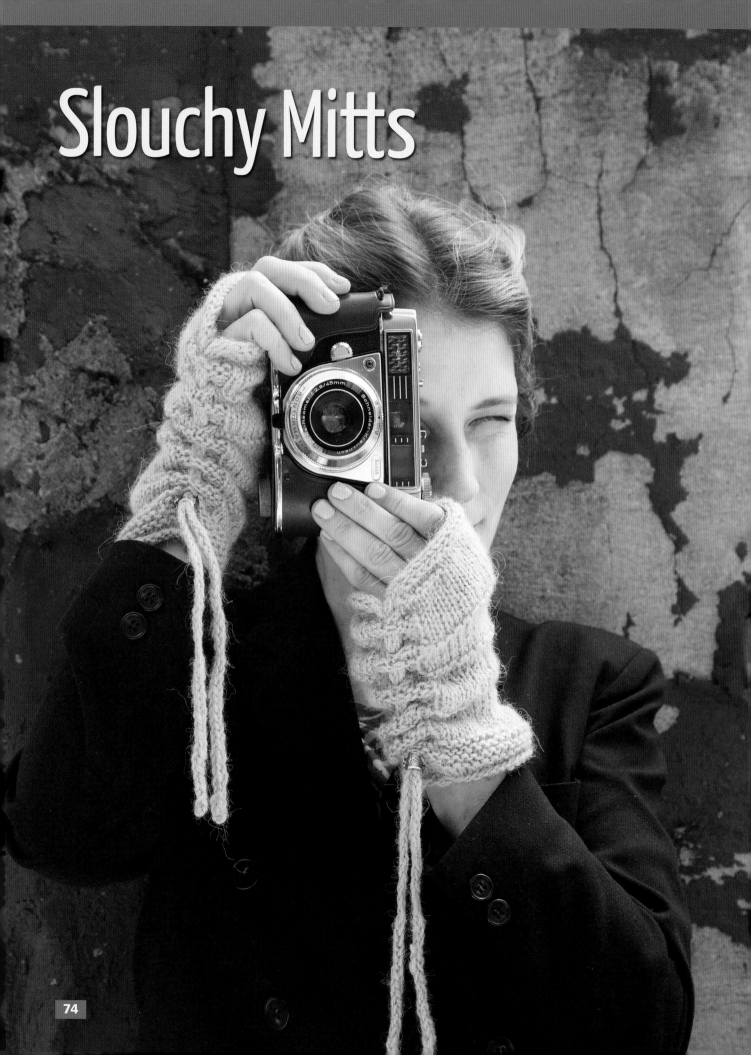

S louchy Mitts are like your favorite pair of sweat-pants: you can cinch them, they're comfy, roomy, and you want to live in them 24/7. Change up the look by using a contrasting color for the I-cord, or using wooden or decorative beads.

FINISHED MEASUREMENTS
Hand circumference: 7¾"/19.5 cm
Length: 9"/23 cm

YARN
Deborah Norville Collection Alpaca Dance by Premier Yarns, DK weight #3 yarn (75% acrylic, 25% alpaca; 371 yd/3.5 oz, 339 m/ 100 g per skein)
• 1 skein #25-16 Silver Fog

NEEDLES AND OTHER MATERIALS
• US 5 (3.75 mm) set of 5 double-pointed needles (dpns)
• 2 extra US 5 (3.75 mm) dpns
• Two ⅜"/1 cm beads
• Tapestry needle
• Stitch markers
• Smooth waste yarn

GAUGE
20 sts x 26 rows in St st = 4"/10 cm square
Be sure to check your gauge!

Right Mitt

CO 38 sts. Divide sts evenly between 4 dpns and join to work in the rnd. Pm for beg of rnd.

Cuff
Rnds 1–4: Knit.
Rnd 5: P5, pm, purl to end.
Rnd 6: Purl to m, knit to end.
Rnd 7: P1, p2tog, yo, purl to end.
Rnd 8: Rep Rnd 6.
Rnd 9: Rep Rnd 5.

Wrist
Rnds 1 & 2: Knit.
Rnd 3: K1, k2tog, yo, k2, p8, knit to last 8 sts, purl to end.
Rnds 4 & 5: Rep Rnd 1.
Rnds 6 & 7: Purl to m, knit to end.
Rnd 8: P1, p2tog, yo, purl to end.
Rnds 9 & 10: Rep Rnds 6 & 7.

Rnds 11 & 12: Knit.
Rnd 13: K1, k2tog, yo, k2, p5, knit to last 5 sts, purl to end.
Rnds 14 & 15: Rep Rnds 11 &12.
Rnds 16–20: Rep Rnds 6–10.
Rnds 21 & 22: Knit to end.
Rnd 23: K1, k2tog, yo, k2, p6, knit to last 6 sts, purl to end.
Rnds 24 & 25: Rep Rnds 21& 22.

Thumb Gusset

Rnd 1: Purl to m, k19, pm for Thumb, m1L, pm, knit to end—1 st inc'd.

Rnd 2: Purl to first m, knit to end.

Rnd 3: P1, p2tog, yo, p2, knit to Thumb m, m1L, k1, m1R, knit to end—2 sts inc'd; 3 Thumb sts.

Rnd 4: Rep Rnd 2.

Rnd 5: Purl to first m, knit to Thumb m, m1L, k3, m1R, knit to end—2 sts inc'd; 5 Thumb sts.

Rnd 6: Knit to end.

Rnd 7: Knit to Thumb m, m1L, k5, m1R, knit to end—2 sts inc'd; 7 Thumb sts.

Rnd 8: K1, k2tog, yo, k2, p10, knit to last 10 sts, purl to end.

Rnd 9: Knit to Thumb m, m1L, k7, m1R, knit to end—2 sts inc'd; 9 Thumb sts.

Rnd 10: Rep Rnd 6.

Rnd 11: Purl to first m, knit to end.

Rnd 12: P1, p2tog, yo, p2, knit to Thumb m, m1L, k9, m1R, knit to end—2 sts inc'd; 11 Thumb sts.

Rnd 13: P1, p2tog, yo, p2, knit to end.

Rnd 14: Rep Rnd 11.

Rnd 15: Purl to first m, knit to Thumb m, m1L, k11, m1R, knit to end—2 sts inc'd; 13 Thumb sts.

Hand

Rnd 1: Knit to Thumb m, remove m, place Thumb sts on waste yarn, remove other Thumb m, knit to end—38 sts rem.

Rnd 2: Knit to end.

Rnd 3: K1, k2tog, yo, k2, p9, knit to last 9 sts, purl to end.

Rnds 4 & 5: Rep Rnd 2.

Rnds 6–15: Rep Rnds 6–15 of Wrist.

Rnd 16: Purl.

Sl first 2 sts of rnd to RH needle. Break yarn, leaving live sts on needles.

I-Cord Edging/Ties

CO 2 sts to extra dpn. * Slide sts to other end of needle and place in left hand, k2; rep from * until I-cord measures 10"/25.5 cm.

I-Cord Bind-off

Slip 2 I-cord sts to LH Mitt needle. * K2, k2tog tbl (1 st bound off), slip these 3 sts back to LH needle; rep from * until all sts have been bound off—3 sts rem on needle. Slip these 3 sts back to LH needle, k1, k2tog—2 sts rem. Work 10" of I-cord on these 2 sts. BO.

Thumb

Divide held Thumb sts between 3 dpns. Beg at center of Thumb gap, pick up and knit 2 sts, k13, pick up and knit 1—16 sts.

Dec rnd: K1, k2tog, knit to last 3 sts, ssk, k1—14 sts rem. Knit 4 rnds. BO all sts loosely pwise.

Left Mitt

Work as for Right Mitt to Thumb Gusset.

Thumb Gusset

Rnd 1: Purl to m, k14, pm for Thumb, m1L, pm, knit to end—1 st inc'd.

Work remainder of Left Mitt as for Right Mitt.

Finishing

For each mitt, hold both 10" lengths of I-cord together as one and weave in and out of the eyelets. Thread I-cords through bead. Cinch Mitt to desired slouchiness.

Weave in loose ends.

Boutros the Beetle

Did you know there are well over 350,000 discovered species of beetles on the planet and counting? Allow me to introduce the newest member of the beetle family, Boutros. Boutros does not prey upon plants, sneak into your house, or do any of the creepy-crawly things that other beetles do. He exists upon these fingerless mitts for the sole purpose of entertaining you with his attractive knitted exoskeleton. Enjoy!

FINISHED MEASUREMENTS
Hand circumference: 8"/20.5 cm
Length: 7"/18 cm

YARN
Deborah Norville Collection Serenity Sock Solids by Premier Yarns, superfine weight #1 yarn (50% superwash merino, 25% rayon from bamboo, 25% nylon; 230 yd/1.75 oz, 210 m/50 g per skein)
• 1 skein #DN 150-04 Purple (CC)
• 1 skein #DN 150-08 Hot Lime (MC)

NEEDLES AND OTHER MATERIALS
• US 2 (2.25 mm) set of 5 double-pointed needles (dpn)
• Tapestry needle
• Stitch markers
• Waste yarn

GAUGE
8 sts x 8 rows in stranded knitting = 4"/10 cm square
Be sure to check your gauge!

NOTES
• See page 103 for a tutorial on backward-loop cast-on and page 112 for a tutorial on stranded knitting.

Thumb

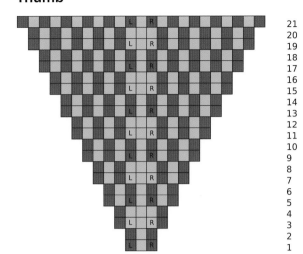

Key

⊡ purl

☐ knit

Ⓛ make 1 left

Ⓡ make 1 right

⬜ MC

⬛ CC

Left Mitt

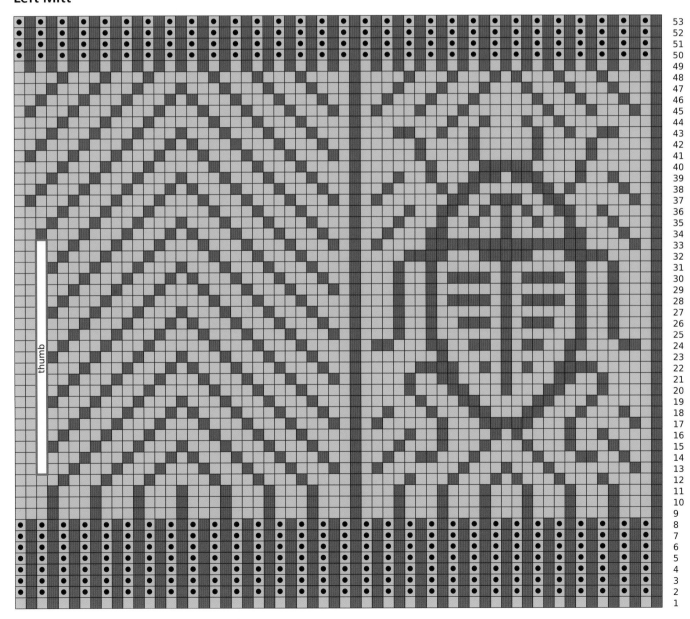

Right Mitt

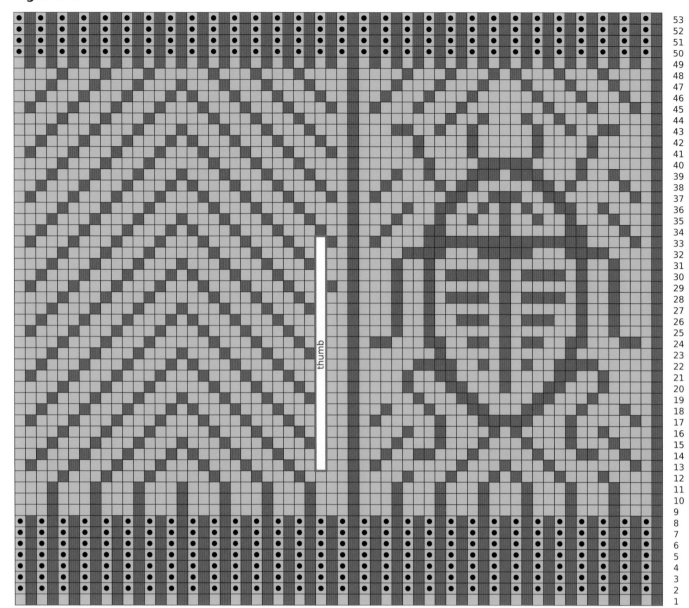

Key

⊡ purl

☐ knit

L make 1 left

R make 1 right

▨ MC

■ CC

Right Mitt

CO 60 sts. Divide evenly between 4 dpns and join to work in the rnd.

Cuff

Work Rows 1–8 of Right Mitt chart.

Hand

Work Rows 9–12 of Right Mitt chart.

Thumb Gusset

Inc rnd: Work 31 sts of Row 13 of chart, pm, work Row 1 of Thumb chart, pm, work to end—2 sts inc'd.

Next rnd: Work even in patt.

Work Rows 15–33 of Right Mitt chart, working Thumb Gusset chart between markers—23 Thumb sts.

Next rnd: Work Row 34 of Right Mitt chart to m, remove m, place Thumb sts on waste yarn, remove m, CO 1 st using backward-loop method and MC, work to end—60 sts rem.

Cont in patt through Row 53 of Right Mitt chart. Break MC. With CC, knit 1 rnd. BO all sts pwise.

Thumb

Place held Thumb sts evenly onto 3 dpns. Beg at center of Thumb gap, with MC, pick up and knit 2 sts, [k1 with CC, k1 with MC] to last st, k1 with CC, pick up and knit 1 with CC—26 sts.

Next rnd: With CC, k2tog, work in patt to last 3 sts, ssk with CC, k1 with MC—24 sts rem.

Work 2 rnds in patt. Break MC. With CC, knit 1 rnd. BO all sts pwise

Left Mitt

CO 60 sts. Divide sts evenly between 4 dpns and join to work in the rnd.

Cuff

Work Rows 1–8 of Left Mitt chart.

Hand

Work Rows 9–12 of Left Mitt chart.

Thumb Gusset

Inc rnd: Work 57 sts of Row 13 of Left Mitt chart, pm, work Row 1 of Thumb chart, pm, work to end—2 sts inc'd.

Next rnd: Work even in patt.

Work Rows 15–33 of Left Mitt chart, working Thumb chart bet markers—23 Thumb sts.

Next rnd: Work Row 34 of Left Mitt chart to m, remove m, place Thumb sts on waste yarn, remove m, CO 1 st using backward lp method and MC, work to end—60 sts rem.

Cont in patt through Row 53 of Left Mitt chart. Break MC. With CC, knit 1 rnd. Bind off all sts, pwise.

Work Thumb as for Right Mitt.

Finishing

Weave in loose ends. Wet block to even out stranded knitting.

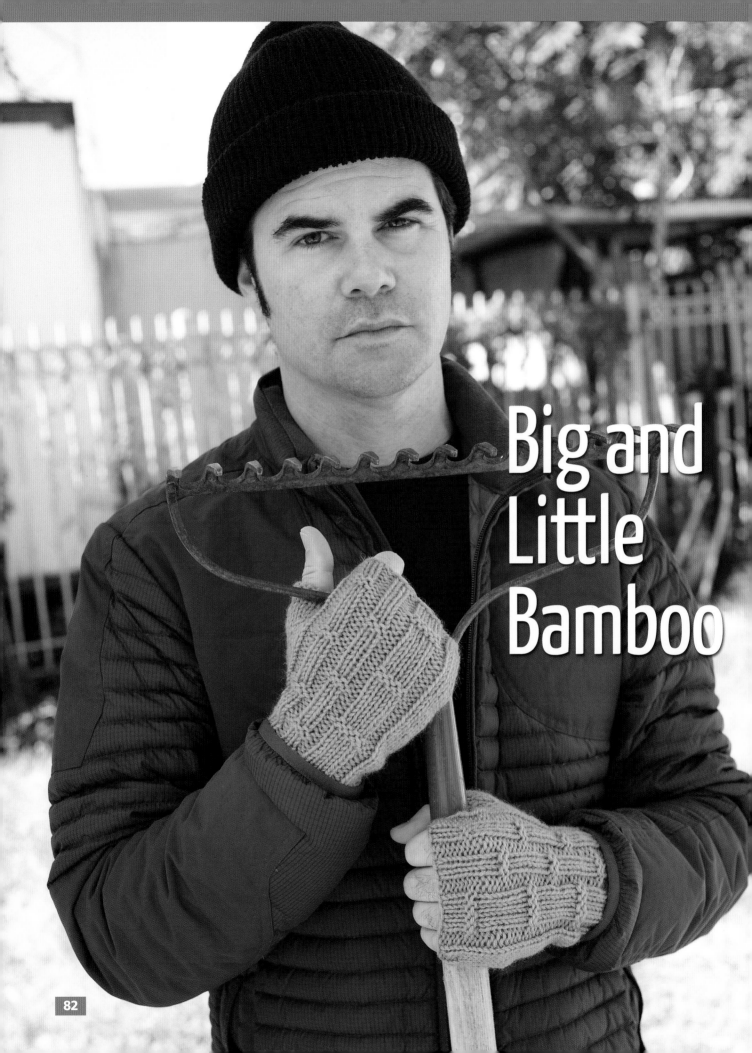

Big and
Little
Bamboo

A simple knit-purl texture pattern and the perfect leafy green color come together to create these unisex mitts. The bamboo "stalks" are very stretchy, making it easy for each size to accommodate a wide variety of hands.

FINISHED MEASUREMENTS

Hand circumference: 6 (7)"/15 (18 cm) unstretched;
  8½ (9½)"/21.5 (24) cm stretched
Length: 7 (8)"/18 (20.5) cm

YARN

Premier Yarns Wool Worsted, medium worsted weight #4 yarn (100% wool; 186 yd/3.5 oz, 170 m/ 100 g per skein)
• 1 skein #35-112 Gecko Green

NEEDLES AND OTHER MATERIALS

• US 6 (4 mm) set of 5 double-pointed needles (dpns)
• Tapestry needle
• Stitch markers

Right Mitt

12
11
10
9
8
7
6
5
4
3
2
1

Left Mitt

12
11
10
9
8
7
6
5
4
3
2
1

Key

☐ knit

▣ purl

Rep Rows 1–12 for patt

GAUGE

18 sts x 24 rows in St st = 4"/10 cm square
Be sure to check your gauge!

NOTES

• When casting on in Thumb Gusset section, use the backward-loop method (see page 103 for a tutorial).

Right Mitt

CO 31 (35) sts. Divide evenly between 4 dpns and join to work in the rnd.

Cuff

Rnd 1: P0 (1), k1, p1, k4, [p1, k2] 2 times, [p1, k1] to last 1 (2) sts, p1, k0 (1).
Rep this rnd 6 more times.

Hand

Setup rnd: K1 (2), pm, pfb, k4, pfb, [k2, pfb] 2 times, pm, k8, kfb, knit to end—36 (40) sts.
Rnd 1: Knit to m, work Row 1 of Right Mitt chart to m, knit to end.
Rnds 2–6 (8): Knit to m, work next row of chart to m, knit to end.

Thumb Gusset

Rnd 1: Work in patt across 20 (22) sts, pm for Thumb, m1L, pm, knit to end—1 st inc'd.
Rnd 2: Work in patt to Thumb m, knit to end.
Rnd 3: Work in patt to m, CO 1 st, k1, CO 1 st, knit to end —2 sts inc'd.
Rnd 4: Work in patt to m, knit to end.
Rnd 5 (inc): Work in patt to m, CO 1 st, knit to m, CO 1 st, knit to end—2 sts inc'd.
Rnd 6: Work in patt to m, knit to end.
Rep last 2 rnds 5 (6) more times—15 (17) Thumb sts.
Next rnd: Work in patt to m, remove m, sl Thumb sts to waste yarn, remove m, knit to end—36 (40) sts rem.
Cont in patt for 13 (15) more rnds, through Row 11 (5) of Right Mitt chart.
Next rnd: Work in patt across 18 (20) sts, [k2 (3), k2tog, k3, k2tog] twice—32 (36) sts rem.

Top Edging

Rnd 1: P0 (1), k1, p2, k4, [p2, k2] 2 times, p2, [k1, p1] to last 3 (2) sts, k1 (0), p2tog—31 (35) sts rem.
Rnd 2: P0 (1), k1, p2, k4, [p2, k2] 2 times, p2, [k1, p1] to last 0 (1) st, k0 (1).
Rep last rnd 1 more time.
BO all sts loosely in patt.

Thumb

Place held Thumb sts evenly onto 3 dpns. Beg at center of Thumb gap, pick up and knit 2 sts, k15 (17), pick up and knit 1—18 (20) sts.
Dec rnd: K1, k2tog, knit to last 2 sts, ssk—16 (18) sts rem.
Knit 2 rnds. BO all sts loosely pwise.

Left Mitt

CO 31 (35) sts. Divide evenly between 4 dpns and join to work in the rnd.

Cuff

Rnd 1: P0 (1), k1, [p1, k2] 2 times, p1, k4, [p1, k1] to last 1 (2) sts, p1, k0 (1).

Rep this rnd 6 more times.

Hand

Setup rnd: K1 (2), pm, pfb, [k2, pfb] twice, k4, pfb, pm, k8, kfb, knit to end—36 (40) sts.

Rnd 1: Knit to m, work Row 1 of Left Mitt chart to m, knit to end.

Rnds 2–6 (8): Knit to m, work next row of chart to m, knit to end.

Thumb Gusset

Rnd 1: Work in patt to last 2 sts, pm for Thumb, m1L, pm, knit to end—1 st inc'd.

Comp Thumb Gusset as for Right Mitt, using Left Mitt chart.

Cont in patt for 13 (15) more rnds, through Row 11 (5) of Left Mitt chart.

Next rnd: Work in patt across 18 (20) sts, [k2 (3), k2tog, k3, k2tog] twice—32 (36) sts rem.

Top Edging

Rnd 1: P0 (1), k1, [p2, k2] 2 times, p2, k4, p2, [k1, p1] to last 3 (2) sts, k1 (0), p2tog—31 (35) sts rem.

Rnd 2: P0 (1), k1, [p2, k2] 2 times, p2, k4, p2, [k1, p1] to last 0 (1) st(s), k0 (1).

Rep this rnd 1 more time.

BO all sts loosely in patt.

Thumb

Comp as for Right Mitt.

Finishing

Weave in loose ends and block.

Swedish Mittens

Prepare to have toasty hands with these mittens. Swedish Mittens are worked from the bottom up in 2-color stranded knitting, creating a warm, insulated fabric for your hands. After the main mitten is knit, stitches are picked up and an extra outer cuff is worked for maximum protection from Old Man Winter. Don't be fooled by the little green dots in the center of each colorwork motif. The stranded knitting really is only two colors at a time. These extra pops of color are added as an afterthought using a simple embroidery technique.

FINISHED MEASUREMENTS
Hand circumference: 7½ (8½)"/19 (21.5) cm
Length: 10 (10½)"/25.5 (26.5) cm

YARN
Deborah Norville Collection Alpaca Dance by Premier Yarns, DK weight #3 yarn (75% acrylic, 25% alpaca; 371 yd/3.5 oz, 942 m/100 g per skein)
- 1 skein #25-04 Red Haze (A)
- 1 skein #25-01 Soft White (B)
- 1 skein #25-07 Lemon Lime (C)

NEEDLES AND OTHER MATERIALS
- US 4 (3.5 mm) set of 5 double-pointed needles (dpns)
- 4 spare US 4 (3.5mm) or smaller dpns
- Tapestry needle
- Stitch markers
- Waste yarn

GAUGE
24 sts x 25 rnds in stranded colorwork = 4"/10 cm square
Be sure to check your gauge!

NOTES
- Use a knitted cast-on for the I-Cord Bind-off (see page 101 for a tutorial).
- See page 112 for a tutorial on stranded knitting.

Top

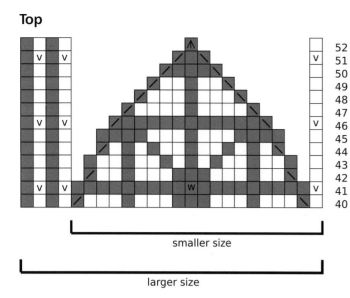

52
51
50
49
48
47
46
45
44
43
42
41
40

smaller size

larger size

Hand

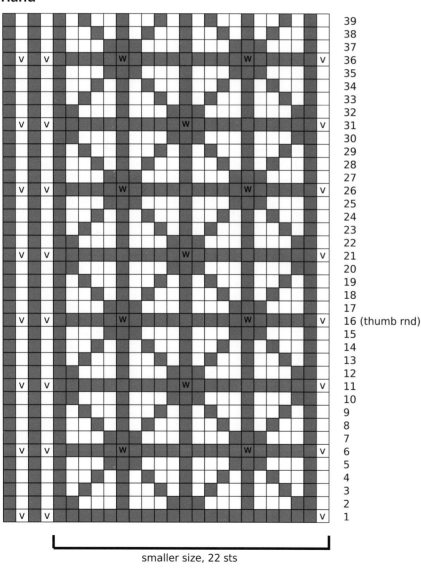

39
38
37
36
35
34
33
32
31
30
29
28
27
26
25
24
23
22
21
20
19
18
17
16 (thumb rnd)
15
14
13
12
11
10
9
8
7
6
5
4
3
2
1

smaller size, 22 sts

larger size, 26 sts

Right Mitten

With A, CO 32 (38) sts. Divide evenly between 4 dpns and join to work in the rnd.

Inner Cuff

Rnd 1: * K1, p1; rep from * to end.
Rep Rnd 1 until Inner Cuff measures 2½"/6.5 cm from CO edge.

Smaller Size Only

Inc rnd: K1, m1L, [k3, m1L] 9 times, [k2, m1] twice—12 sts inc'd; 44 sts.

Larger Size Only

Inc rnd: * K1, m1L, k2, [m1L, k3] 5 times, m1L, k2, m1L, k1; rep from * once more—14 sts inc'd; 52 sts.

Hand

Knit 1 rnd.
Attach B. With B, knit 1 rnd.
Work Rows 1–15 of Hand chart—chart will be repeated twice across rnd.
Rnd 16 (Thumb rnd): Work Row 16 of chart across 24 (28) sts, with waste yarn, k6 (8), slip these 6 (8) sts back to LH needle, work in patt to end.
Cont in patt through Row 39 of Hand chart.
Work Rows 40–50 (52) of Top chart. BO rem 12 sts using A.

Key

☐ with A, knit

▨ with B, knit

◥ ssk

◢ k2tog

Ʌ sl 1, k2tog, psso

ⓥ sl 1 pwise wyib

ⓦ indicates st to Wrap in Finishing section

Embroidery

Cut two 30"/76 cm pieces of C. Thread 1 piece through tapestry needle. Wrap yarn twice around each st indicated by W symbol on Hand chart on back of mitten. Rep with rem piece of C on palm of mitten.

Outer Cuff

With A and WS facing, beg at side opposite Thumb, pick up and knit 48 (54) sts along cast-on edge of Inner Cuff. Divide evenly among 4 dpns and join to work in the rnd.

Note: It will make the work easier to pull the mitten inside out through working needles.

Knit 1 rnd. Attach B.

Next rnd: * With A, k2, with B, k1; rep from * to end.

Rep this rnd 11 more times. Break A and B.

Dec rnd: With C, * k10 (25), k2tog; rep from * to end—44 (52) sts rem.

Pick up 44 (52) sts from Hand by inserting 4 dpns through front loop of each st of the B rnd just before Row 1 of chart. These are the "Back" needles; the Cuff needles are the "Front" needles.

I-Cord Bind-off

CO 2 sts to first st on Front LH needle. * K2, sl next st to Front RH needle, sl this st to Back LH needle, k3tog tbl (1 st bound off from both front and back needles), sl 3 sts from RH needle to Front LH needle; rep from * until all sts from front and back needles have been bound off, BO rem 3 sts in the normal way.

Thumb

Hold 2 dpns parallel; with a third dpn, carefully remove waste yarn from held Thumb sts, 1 st at a time. Place upper 6 (8) sts on one dpn, and lower 6 (8) sts on the other.

Rnd 1: With B, pick up and knit 2 sts from side of Thumb gap; working across sts from dpn, [with A, k1, with B, k1] 3 (4) times; with A, pick up and knit 2 sts from other side of Thumb gap; working across sts from other dpn, [with B, k1, with A, k1] 3 (4) times—16 (20) sts.

Dec rnd: With B, k2tog, [with A, k1, with B, k1] 3 (4) times, with A, k2tog, [with B, k1, with A, k1] 3 (4) times —2 sts dec'd; 14 (18) sts rem.

Next rnd: * With B, k1, with A, k1; rep from * to end.

Rep this rnd until Thumb meas 2¼ (2½)"/5.5 (6) cm.

Dec rnd: * With B, ssk, with A, k2tog; rep from * to last 2 (0) sts, end with B, ssk—7 (8) sts rem. Break yarn, thread through tapestry needle, and pass through rem live sts. Pull tight, fasten off.

Left Mitten

Work as for Right Mitten to Hand.

Hand

Knit 1 rnd.

Attach B. With B, knit 1 rnd.

Work Rows 1–15 of chart.

Next rnd: Work Row 16 of chart to last 7 (14) sts, with waste yarn, k6 (8), slip these 6 (8) sts back to LH needle, work in patt to end.

Comp as for Right Mitten.

Outer Cuff

Comp as for Right Mitten.

Thumb

Hold 2 dpns parallel; with a third dpn, carefully remove waste yarn from held Thumb sts, 1 st at a time. Place upper 6 (8) sts on one dpn, and lower 6 (8) sts on the other.

Rnd 1: With A, pick up and knit 2 sts from side of Thumb gap; working across sts from dpn, [with B, k1, with A, k1] 3 (4) times; with B, pick up and knit 2 sts from other side of Thumb gap; working across sts from other dpn, [with A, k1, with B, k1] 3 (4) times—16 (20) sts.

Dec rnd: With A, k2tog, [with B, k1, with A, k1] 3 (4) times, with B, k2tog, [with A, k1, with B, k1] 3 (4) times —2 sts dec'd; 14 (18) sts rem.

Next rnd: * With A, k1, with B, k1; rep from * to end.

Rep this rnd until Thumb meas 2¼ (2½)"/5.5 (6) cm.

Dec rnd: * With A, ssk, with B, k2tog; rep from * to last 2 (0) sts, end with A, ssk—7 sts rem. Break yarn, thread through tapestry needle, and pass through rem live sts. Pull tight, fasten off.

Finishing

Weave in ends.

Go Your
Own Way

A tightly twisted acrylic yarn makes crossed stitches pop to the surface in these slightly asymmetric mitts. The right and left hands are mirror images of each other throughout most of the cable chart. But something unusual happens. Righty and Lefty have different ideas and they decide to take separate paths.

FINISHED MEASUREMENTS
Hand circumference: 7 (8½, 9¾)"/18 (21.5, 25) cm
Length: 6¼ (6¾, 7¼)"/16 (17, 18.5) cm

YARN
Premier Yarns Primo, fine weight #2 yarn, (100% acrylic anti-pilling fiber; 273 yd/3.5 oz, 693 m/100 g per skein)
• 1 skein #28-02 Cream

NEEDLES AND OTHER MATERIALS
• US 3 (3.25 mm) set of 5 double-pointed needles (dpns)
• US 4 (3.5 mm) set of 5 dpns
• Cable needle
• Tapestry needle
• Stitch markers
• Waste yarn

GAUGE
23 sts x 30 rows in St st = 4"/10 cm square
Be sure to check your gauge!

STITCH GUIDE
2x2 Right Cross (2x2 RC)
Sl next 2 sts to cn and hold in back, k2 from LH needle, k2 from cn.

2x2 Left Cross (2x2 LC)
Sl next 2 sts to cn and hold in front, k2 from LH needle, k2 from cn.

Back of left mitt

Right Mitt

Left Mitt

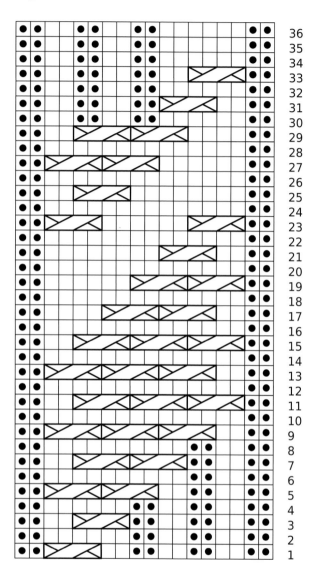

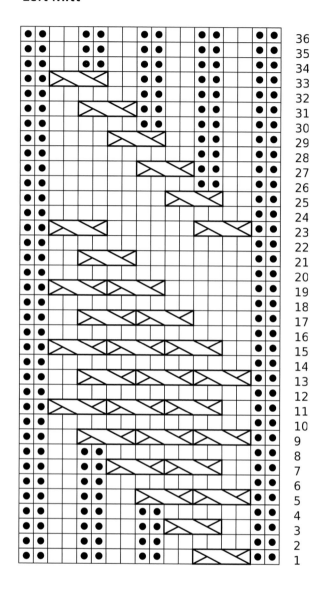

Key

☐ knit

⊡ purl

▨ 2x2 RC

▧ 2x2 LC

Right Mitt

With smaller needles, CO 44 (52, 60) sts. Divide evenly between 4 dpns and join to work in the rnd.

Cuff

Smallest & Largest Sizes Only

Rnd 1: P1, * k2, p2; rep from * to last 3 sts, k2, p1. Rep this rnd 6 more times.

Medium Size Only

Rnd 1: K1, * p2, k2; rep from * to last 3 sts, p2, k1. Rep this rnd 6 more times.

Hand

Switch to larger needles.

Setup rnd: K3 (5, 7), pm, work Row 1 of Right Mitt chart over 18 sts, pm, knit to end.

Next rnd: Knit to m, work Row 2 of chart to m, knit to end.

Cont in established patt through Row 14 of chart.

Thumb Gusset

Rnd 1: Knit to m, work in patt to m, k5 (7, 9), pm for Thumb, m1L, pm, knit to end—1 st inc'd.

Rnd 2: Work in patt to Thumb m, knit to end.

Rnd 3: Work in patt to Thumb m, m1L, knit to m, m1R, knit to end—2 sts inc'd.

Rnd 4: Work in patt to Thumb m, knit to end.

Rep last 2 rnds 6 (7, 8) more times—15 (17, 19) Thumb sts.

Next rnd: Work in patt to Thumb m, remove m, sl Thumb sts to waste yarn, remove m, knit to end—42 (50, 58) sts rem.

Next rnd: Knit to m, work Row 31 (33, 35) of chart to m, knit to end.

Cont in patt for 5 (3, 1) more rnd(s), through Row 36 of chart. Cont in patt, repeating Row 36 of chart bet markers for 2 (4, 6) more rnds.

Upper Edging

Switch to smaller needles.

Smallest & Largest Sizes Only

Rnd 1: P1, * k2, p2; rep from * to last 3 sts, k2, p1. Repeat this rnd 3 more times.

Medium Size Only

Rnd 1: K1, * p2, k2; rep from * to last 3 sts, p2, k1. Repeat this rnd 3 more times.

All Sizes

Knit 2 rnds. BO all sts loosely.

Thumb

Place held Thumb sts onto 3 dpns. Beg at center of Thumb gap, pick up and knit 2 sts, k15 (17, 19), pick up and knit 1—18 (20, 22) sts.

Dec rnd: K1, k2tog, knit to last 2 sts, ssk—16 (18, 20) sts rem.

Knit 2 rnds. BO all sts loosely.

Left Mitt

Work as for Right Mitt to Thumb Gusset, using Left Mitt chart.

Thumb Gusset

Rnd 1: Knit to m, work in patt to m, knit to last 2 sts, pm for Thumb, m1L, pm, knit to end—1 st inc'd.

Rnd 2: Work in patt to Thumb m, knit to end.

Comp remainder of Left Mitt as for Right Mitt.

Finishing

Weave in loose ends.

Mitered
Mitts

These cute little mitts may look complicated, but they are nothing more than a couple of squares sewn together. Instead of working the squares from side to side, you will work them from the outside in. The cast-on stitches comprise two of the four sides of each square. Central decreases are worked on every right-side row to give the squares their shape. Try using a striping yarn for the A color, as shown. Be sure to choose a B color that contrasts with A for defined ridges and lines.

FINISHED MEASUREMENTS
Hand circumference: 7 (7¾, 8¾)"/18 (19.5, 22) cm
Length: 4¼ (4¾, 5)"/11 (12, 12.5) cm

YARN
Deborah Norville Collection Serenity Sock by Premier Yarns, superfine weight #1 yarn (50% superwash merino, 25% rayon from bamboo, 25% nylon; 230 yd/1.75 oz, 210 m/ 50 g per skein)
• 1 skein #123-01 Pink Sugar (A)
Deborah Norville Collection Serenity Sock Solids by Premier Yarns, superfine weight #1 yarn (50% superwash merino wool, 25% rayon from bamboo, 25% nylon; 230 yd/1.75 oz, 210 m/ 50 g per skein)
• 1 skein #150-11 Charcoal (B)

NEEDLES AND OTHER MATERIALS
• US 2 (2.75 mm) set of 5 double-pointed needles (dpns)
• Tapestry needle
• Removable stitch marker

GAUGE
28 sts x 48 rows in Garter st = 4"/10 cm square
Be sure to check your gauge!

NOTES
• When working the Hand section, move the marker up each row, keeping it on the centermost stitch.
• To achieve a pair of matching mitts, begin both Backs of Hands and both Palms in the same color repeat of the yarn.
• For the Lower Edging/Ties, use a knitted cast-on (see page 101 for a tutorial).

Back of Hand/Palm

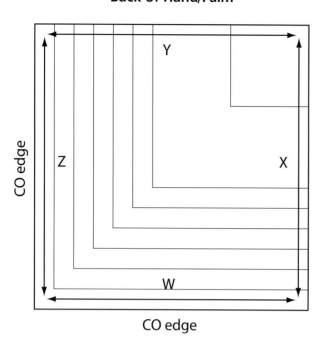

CO edge

CO edge

Right Mitt

Back of Hand

With A, CO 51 (57, 63) sts.

Setup row (WS): With A, k25 (28, 31), k1, place removable m on st just knit, k25 (28, 31).

Section 1

Row 1 (RS): With A, knit to 1 st before marked st, sl 1, k2tog, psso, knit to end—2 sts dec'd.

Row 2: With A, knit.

Rows 3 & 4: Rep Rows 1 & 2.

Row 5: With B, rep Row 1.

Row 6: With B, purl.

Rep these 6 rows 2 (3, 4) more times—33 sts rem.

Section 2

Row 1: With A, knit to 1 st before marked st, sl 1, k2tog, psso, knit to end—2 sts dec'd.

Row 2: With A, knit.

Row 3: With B, rep Row 1.

Row 4: With B, purl.

Rep Rows 1–4 two more times—21 sts rem.

Rep Rows 3 & 4 one more time—19 sts rem. Break B.

Section 3

Row 1: With A, knit to 1 st bef marked st, sl 1, k2tog, psso, knit to end—2 sts dec'd.

Row 2: With A, knit.

Row 3: Rep Row 1.

Row 4: With A, purl.

Rep Rows 1–4 two more times—7 sts rem.

Rep Rows 1 & 2 one more time—5 sts rem.

Rep Row 1 one more time—3 sts rem.

K3tog over next WS row, fasten off last st.

Palm

Comp as for Back of Hand.

Seams

Sew X edge of Back of Hand to Y edge of Palm—Outer Seam formed.

Beg at center of CO edge, sew Z edge of Back of Hand to W edge of Palm along 1¾ (2, 2¼)"/4.5 (5, 5.5) cm, leave 1¼ (1½, 1¾)"/3 (4, 4.5) cm unsewn for Thumb-hole, sew remainder of edge—Inner Seam formed.

Left Mitt

Work Back of Hand and Palm as for Right Mitt. Sew together as for Right Mitt, reversing Back of Hand and Palm.

Finishing

Top Edging

With A, beg at Inner Seam, pick up and knit 48 (54, 60) sts evenly around Top edge of Mitt. Divide evenly between 4 dpns and join to work in the rnd.

Rnd 1: Purl.

Rnd 2: Knit.

Rep these 2 rnds 2 more times. BO all sts loosely pwise.

Lower Edging/Ties

With B, CO 48 (52, 56) sts, beg at Outer Seam, pick up and knit 44 (50, 56) sts evenly around Lower edge of Mitt, CO 48 (52, 56) sts—140 (154, 168) sts.

Purl 1 row. Knit 1 row. Purl 1 row. BO all sts kwise.

Weave in ends. Tie ends of Lower Edging in a bow.

How to Use This Book

Yarn

The specific yarn used is listed in the materials section for each project. If the yarn used is not available to you or you'd like to try something different, go for it! You'll want to take note of two important things: yarn weight and gauge.

The CYC (Craft Yarn Council of America) classifies yarn weight as ranging from 0 Lace-weight to 6 Super Bulky (see chart below). The weights of yarn used in this book range from 1 Superfine to 4 Medium. If you'd like to use a different yarn than is called for in a pattern, be sure to pick one that is the same weight as the yarn used.

Standard Yarn Weight System

Categories of yarn, gauge ranges, and recommended needle and hook sizes

Yarn Weight Symbol & Category Names	**0** Lace	**1** Super Fine	**2** Fine	**3** Light	**4** Medium	**5** Bulky	**6** Super Bulky
Type of Yarns in Category	Fingering 10 count crochet thread	Sock, Fingering, Baby	Sport, Baby	DK, Light Worsted	Worsted, Afghan, Aran	Chunky, Craft, Rug	Bulky, Roving
Knit Gauge Range* in Stockinette Stitch to 4 inches	33 –40** sts	27–32 sts	23–26 sts	21–24 sts	16–20 sts	12–15 sts	6–11 sts
Recommended Needle in Metric Size Range	1.5–2.25 mm	2.25–3.25 mm	3.25–3.75 mm	3.75–4.5 mm	4.5–5.5 mm	5.5–8 mm	8 mm and larger
Recommended Needle U.S. Size Range	000 to 1	1 to 3	3 to 5	5 to 7	7 to 9	9 to 11	11 and larger
Crochet Gauge* Ranges in Single Crochet to 4 inch	32-42 double crochets**	21–32 sts	16–20 sts	12–17 sts	11–14 sts	8–11 sts	5–9 sts
Recommended Hook in Metric Size Range	Steel*** 1.6–1.4mm Regular hook 2.25 mm	2.25–3.5 mm	3.5–4.5 mm	4.5–5.5 mm	5.5–6.5 mm	6.5–9 mm	9 mm and larger
Recommended Hook U.S. Size Range	Steel*** 6, 7, 8 Regular hook B–1	B–1 to E–4	E–4 to 7	7 to I–9	I–9 to K–10½	K–10½ to M–13	M–13 and larger

* GUIDELINES ONLY: The above reflect the most commonly used gauges and needle or hook sizes for specific yarn categories.

** Lace weight yarns are usually knitted or crocheted on larger needles and hooks to create lacy, openwork patterns. Accordingly, a gauge range is difficult to determine. Always follow the gauge stated in your pattern.

*** Steel crochet hooks are sized differently from regular hooks--the higher the number, the smaller the hook, which is the reverse of regular hook sizing.

This Standards & Guidelines booklet and downloadable symbol artwork are available at: **YarnStandards.com**

Gauge

Gauge, or tension, refers to how many stitches/rows in a particular stitch you should be knitting per inch (for example, 20 sts x 20 rows = 4"/10 cm square in stockinette stitch).

Typically, it is very important to do what is called a gauge swatch—a sample of the size called for in the gauge information, using the yarn and needles you plan to use for the project—to determine if you are getting the correct gauge. If your gauge is too loose (fewer stitches per inch than called for) or too tight (more

stitches per inch), then you need to adjust your needle size. For loose gauge, go down in needle size. If your gauge is too tight, try using a larger needle. For this book, I say forget the gauge swatch (even though I do tell you what the gauge should be for each project)! The beauty of fingerless gloves and mittens is that the projects are all small to begin with, so they're really just big swatches. I recommend casting on for a project to start. If after a couple of inches you see that your gauge is off, start again with the appropriate needle size.

Abbreviations

beg	beginning
bet	between
BO	bind off
cn	cable needle
CO	cast on
comp	complete
cont	continue (continuing)
dec('d)	decrease(d)
dpn(s)	double-pointed needle(s)
inc('d)	increase(d)
k	knit
kfb	knit into front of st, knit into back of same st, slip both sts from LH needle—1 st inc'd
kwise	knitwise
k2tog	knit 2 sts tog—1 st dec'd
k3tog	knit 3 sts tog—2 sts dec'd
LH	left hand
m	marker
maint	maintain(ing)
m1L	make one left
m1P	make one purl
m1R	make one right
opp	opposite
p	purl
patt	pattern
pm	place marker
prev	previous

psso	pass slipped st(s) over
pwise	purlwise
p2sso	pass 2 slipped sts over
p2tog	purl 2sts tog—1 st dec'd
rem	remain(ing)
rep	repeat
RH	right hand
rnd	round
RS	right side
sl	slip
ssk	sl next 2 sts one at a time, kwise; sl sts back to LH needle and k2tog tbl—1 st dec'd
ssp	slip next 2 sts one at a time, kwise; sl sts back to LH needle and p2tog tbl—1 st dec'd.
sssk	sl next 3 sts one at a time, kwise; sl sts back to LH needle and k3tog tbl—2 sts dec'd
st(s)	stitch(es)
St st	stockinette stitch
tbl	through the back loop(s)
tog	together
WS	wrong side
w&t	bring yarn to front of work, sl next st to RH needle, bring yarn to back of work, sl st back to LH needle. To work sts tog with wraps: work to wrapped st, lift wrap over wrapped st so both wrap and st are on LH needle, k2tog (wrap + st); on WS rows, ssp (wrap + st).
yo	yarn over

Sizing

Each pattern in this book indicates its finished hand circumference and length. To determine the size you'd like to make, first ask yourself if the mitt will be for yourself or someone else. If it is for you, measure all the way around your hand just above your thumb. This is your actual hand circumference. In most cases, it is better for your mitt to have no ease or even a little bit of negative ease, meaning the finished mitt should be your actual hand measurement, or a little bit less. A snugly fitting mitt is typically better than one that is too large. If you're making one of the projects as a gift, refer to the following standard measurements for hand circumference:

• Women (small): 6½–7"/16.5–18 cm
• Women (medium): 7½–8"/19–20.5 cm
• Women (large): 8½–9"/21.5–23 cm
• Men (small): 7½–8"/19–20.5 cm
• Men (medium): 8½–9"/21.5–23 cm
• Men (large): 9½–10½"/24–26.5 cm

Reading Charts

Most of the fingerless gloves and mittens in this book are worked in the round, but a few are worked back and forth in rows. When reading a colorwork, cable, or lace chart, it is important that you read the chart going in the correct direction. When working in the round, always work the rows from right to left. When working back and forth in rows, work right-side rows from right to left, and wrong-side rows from left to right. A good reminder of this is to always begin on the side of the chart where the number of the row you are on is and work across. Be sure to consult the chart key, pattern stitch guide, and abbreviations list in the back of this book when reading chart symbols.

For bigger charts with lots of rows, it can be hard to keep track of which row you're on. Try taping a sheet of paper over the chart covering everything below the row you're currently on. Move the paper up each row. Another option is to photocopy the chart and cross out each row as you complete it.

Stitch & Technique Guide

This section covers many of the techniques used in this book but not every single aspect of every pattern. Do not forget there is a wealth of information available on the internet! A quick search of the web and sites like YouTube will result in hundreds of videos and photo tutorials on most anything knitted related you might want to know.

Casting On

Casting on is the beginning of every knitted project. It's a way of making a series of loops or, in some instances, a series of foundation row stitches in which to work your piece. For nearly every pattern in this book you will need a good "basic" cast-on to begin your mitt, mitten, or glove. The knitted cast-on (shown below) is one of these basic cast-ons. It provides a row of beginning stitches that is easy to work into. Another go-to cast-on of mine is the long-tail cast-on (not pictured). You can also use the backward-loop method for beginning any project but this particular cast-on is tedious to work into. For this reason, I recommend either the knitted or long-tail methods for starting your project.

Knitted Cast-On

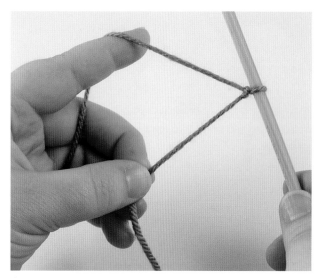

1. Make a slip knot and place it on the needle. Hold this needle in your left hand.

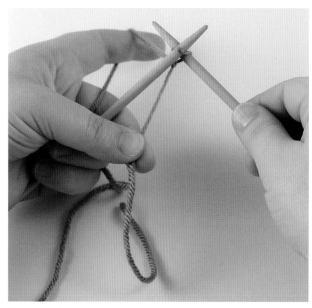

2. Insert the right needle knitwise through the front loop of the stitch.

(continued)

3. Yarn over and bring through the stitch on the left needle.

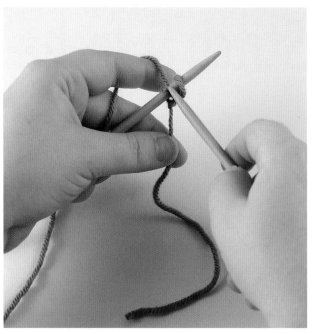

5. Insert the right needle knitwise through the front loop of this new stitch.

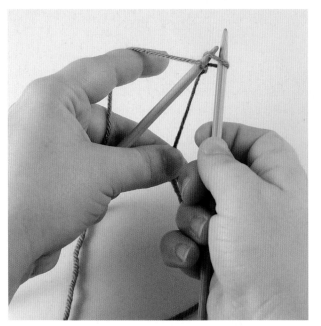

4. Place this stitch back on the left needle—1 stitch cast on.

Repeat steps 3–5 until all stitches have been cast on.

Backward-Loop Cast-On

I am not typically a fan of the backward-loop cast-on when casting on for a project. It is, however, an excellent choice for casting on a small number of stitches within a project. Casting on just a single stitch using this method works well as an increase also, especially in areas where you do not want to skew your work by using the make 1 increase.

1. Make a loop with the working yarn and place it on the right needle backward so it doesn't unwind.

2. Pull loop taut (but not too taut) onto the needle, snugly against the other stitches.

Provisional Crochet Cast-On

A provisional cast-on is as the name implies: it is temporary. There are numerous ways to do a provisional cast-on, and this is the crochet chain version. It is easy to work and requires only a small amount of extra time to do. It is very handy for numerous situations, including going back and binding off using an I-cord bind-off or for joining a turned hem. Be sure to use a smooth, nonsticky, nontextured yarn roughly the same weight as your working yarn for the crocheted chain.

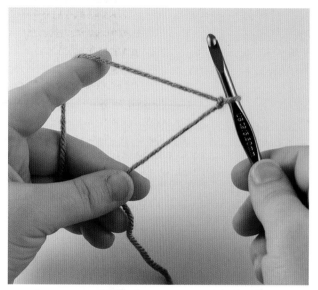

1. Make a slip knot using your waste yarn and place on your crochet hook.

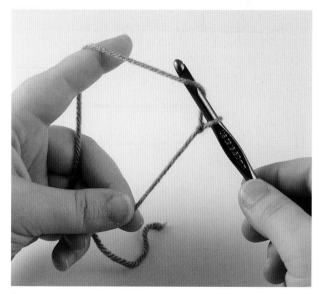

2. Yarn over.

(continued)

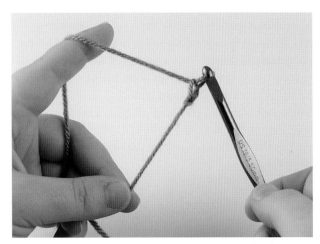

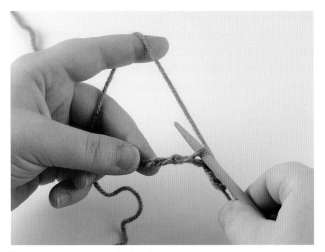

3. Pull the yarn over through the loop on your hook (1 chain made).

4. Repeat steps 2 and 3 until the chain is as long as specified. It is a good idea to make more chains than stitches to be picked up for insurance.

5. Beginning a few chains from one end, insert your needle from front to back through the bottom bump of the crochet chain.

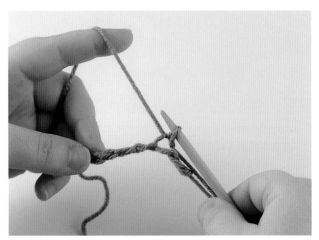

This is what the top of the crochet chain looks like. When your crochet chain is complete, cut your waste yarn, leaving a 6" tail. Secure this tail with a loose knot so the chain does not unravel.

6. Pick up and knit one stitch through this bump using your working yarn.

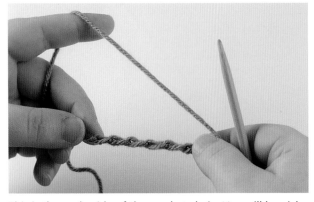

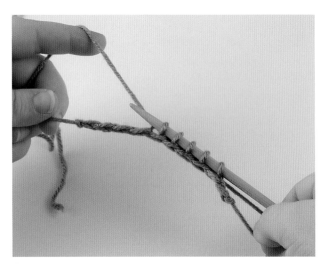

This is the underside of the crochet chain. You will be picking up and knitting stitches through the bottom bump of each chain.

7. Continue to pick up stitches through each successive bottom bump along the crochet chain.

8. After all stitches required have been picked up, continue working as directed, leaving the crochet chain untouched.

10. Pull the waste yarn out of the stitch and place the stitch on your knitting needle.

9. When you have finished, carefully unravel your chain until you reach the first knit stitch.

11. Continue unraveling the chain until all stitches have been placed on your needle.

Increases

Without increases, knitting would be boring and we'd be knitting in straight lines, eh? There are numerous ways to add stitches to your knitting and different reasons for choosing each.

Make 1

The make 1 increase can be worked as either a left- or right-leaning stitch. It is a good increase to use when you want it to be as invisible as possible.

Make 1 Left (m1L)

1. With the left needle, pick up a stitch by inserting the tip from front to back underneath the bar running between the stitch on the right needle and the stitch on the left needle.

2. Knit this stitch through the back leg.

3. One stitch increased.

Make 1 Right (m1R)

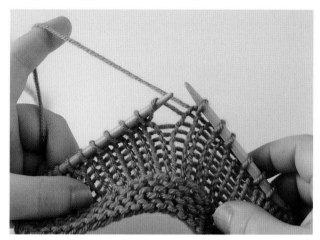

1. With the left needle, pick up a stitch by inserting the tip from back to front underneath the bar running between the stitch on the right needle and the stitch on the left needle.

2. Knit this stitch through the front leg

3. One stitch increased.

Make 1 Purl (m1P)

This is the purl version of the make one increase. Use it on a background of reverse stockinette stitch or when you are increasing on the wrong side of knit fabric.

1. With the left needle, pick up a stitch by inserting the tip from front to back underneath the bar running between the stitch on the right needle and the stitch on the left needle.

2. Purl this stitch through the back leg.

3. One stitch increased

Knit Front and Back (kfb)

The knit front and back increase works well when there are numerous increases to be done because it is relatively simple to perform. It is preferable to use this increase when the increases will not be overly visible.

1. Knit into the front leg of the next stitch; do not remove this stitch from the left needle.

2. Knit into the back leg of the same stitch.

3. Slip both stitches from the needle—one stitch increased.

Knit 1 Below

This is another option that works well if you desire a nearly invisible increase.

1. With the yarn in back of the work, insert the right needle from top to bottom through the purl bump *behind* the next stitch on the left needle.

2. Knit this stitch. One stitch increased.

Purl 1 Below

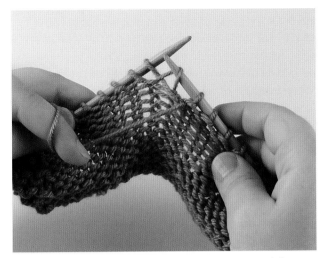

1. With the yarn in front of the work, insert your right needle from top to bottom through the purl bump *behind* the next stitch on the left needle

2. Purl this stitch. One stitch increased.

Decreases

Just as you have options for growing your knitted piece through increasing stitches, there are many alternatives for decreasing stitches as well. Below are the two most frequently used decreases in this book and in knit patterns in general.

Knit 2 Together Decrease (k2tog)
This is a right-leaning decrease.

1. Insert the right needle through the first and second stitches on the left needle, knitwise

Yarn over and bring through the two stitches at the same time.

One stitch decreased.

Slip Slip Knit Decrease (ssk)
This is a left-leaning decrease.

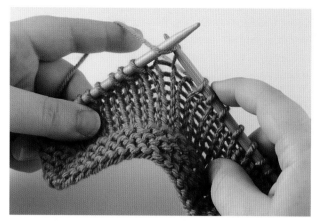

1. Slip the next 2 stitches, knitwise, to the right needle one at a time.

2. Return these stitches back to the left needle, purlwise, one at a time, and knit them together through the back loops.

One stitch decreased.

Intarsia

Intarsia is a method of using two or more colors in knitting. Unlike stranded knitting (see page 112), with this technique you are holding only a single color at a time. Keep in mind you will need a separate length of each color for each section of your work. You can wrap small lengths around bobbins or work directly from the ball.

1. Work to the location of the color change. Bring the new color up and around the old color, putting a twist in the strands.

2. Drop the old color and continue working with the new color.

3. The same principle is used on the wrong side of the work. Cross the strands as shown.

5. Drop the old color and continue working with the new color.

4. Bring the new color up and around the old color, putting a twist in the strands.

Intarsia gives you clean lines between blocks of color.

Stranded Knitting

Also called Fair-Isle knitting, this is a method of using two (or more) colors in knitting. Unlike with intarsia, you are holding both colors throughout the work. These photos show the knitter holding both strands in the same hand. You can also try two-fisted stranded knitting, in which you hold one color in each hand.

1. Knit the next stitch with color A (shown here as white), or whichever color your pattern tells you is next, wrapping A around the needle and leaving the B strand alone in back of the work.

3. If you are working more than 5 stitches in a row with the same color, this will produce long "floats" of the other color on the wrong side of the knitting. Long floats can catch on fingers or other objects and snag your knitting. To avoid these, work across approximately half the stitches of the long (5 stitches or more) section of one color. Bring the working color (shown here as white), up and around the unused color, putting a twist in the strands. Continue working along the row with the working color.

2. Knit the next stitch with color B (shown here as green), wrapping B around the needle and leaving the A strand alone.

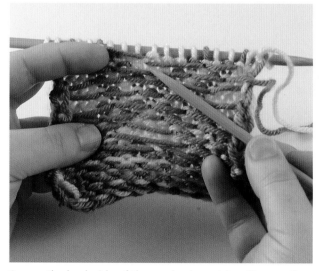

See on the back side of the work where A has "trapped" the B float.

Short Rows

Short rows are a way of shaping fabric, working extra "girth" into your knitting. They are just as the name implies, incomplete rows, short of being a full row. This tutorial covers the basic "wrap and turn" short-row process. This process of wrapping the next stitch will prevent unsightly holes from forming in your knitted fabric.

Wrap and Turn, Knit Side

1. Work to just before the stitch to be wrapped. Bring the yarn to the front of the work.

2. Slip the next stitch to the right needle, purlwise, keeping the yarn in front.

3. Take the yarn to the back.

4. Slip the same stitch back to the left needle, purlwise, keeping the yarn in back. The stitch has now been wrapped.

5. Turn the work. You can see the stitch that was just wrapped on the tip of the right needle. Purl to the end of the row, or to whichever stitch is indicated by your pattern.

Wrap and Turn, Purl Side

1. Work to just before the stitch to be wrapped. Bring the yarn to the back of the work.

2. Slip the next stitch to the right needle, purlwise, keeping the yarn in back.

3. Bring the yarn to the front.

4. Slip the same stitch back to the left needle, purlwise, keeping the yarn in front. The stitch has now been wrapped.

5. Turn the work. You can see the stitch that was just wrapped on the tip of the right needle. Knit to the end of the row, or to whichever stitch is indicated by your pattern.

Working Together Wraps, Knit Side

1. Insert your right needle knitwise through the bottom of the wrap and also through the stitch that was wrapped.

2. Yarn over and knit the wrap together with the stitch.

Working Together Wraps, Purl Side

1. With your right needle, lift the back leg of the wrap onto the left needle.

2. The wrap is now sitting next to the stitch that was wrapped.

3. Purl the stitch together with the wrap.

Making a Box Pleat

This technique will resemble a sewn pleat, where the fabric is folded accordion style. This pleat is worked over 12 stitches.

First Half of Pleat

1. Slip the first 2 stitches on the left needle to a spare dpn or cable needle.

2. Hold this dpn in back.

3. Slip the next 2 stitches on the left needle to a second dpn.

4. Rotate this dpn clockwise 180 degrees.

5. Hold this second dpn between the left needle and the first dpn.

6. Knit 3 stitches together (k3tog) by inserting your right needle through the front leg of each stitch.

7. Yarn over and pull through all 3 stitches.

8. Slide stitches off the left needle. K3tog once more – 2 stitches on the right needle.

Second Half of Pleat

1. Slip the first 2 stitches on the left needle to a dpn. Hold this dpn in front.

2. Slip the next 2 stitches on the left needle to a second dpn. Rotate this dpn counterclockwise 180 degrees.

(continued)

3. Hold this second dpn between the left needle and the first dpn. K3tog twice.

4. One box pleat completed.

Applied Chained Crochet Lines

In this example, we will be working applied chained crochet lines onto columns of reverse stockinette stitch (as in the It's a Plaid Plaid World mitts on page 66). Note the reverse stockinette columns amidst the mostly stockinette fabric.

1. Holding your yarn beneath the fabric, insert your hook from the front through the center of the first stitch.

2. Yarn over.

3. Pull the yarn over through the stitch to the front—
1 loop on the hook.

4. Insert your hook from the front through the center of
the next stitch above the stitch you just went through.

5. Yarn over and pull the yarn through the stitch to the
front—2 loops on the hook.

6. Pull the new loop through the first—1 loop remaining
on the hook.

7. Repeat steps 4–6 until all stitches have been worked.
Cut yarn and pull the end up and through the loop to
secure, then pull the end to the back of the work to be
woven in.

Blocking

Blocking is not just for sports! It's often a very important step in finishing your knitted project. Blocking refers to the process of smoothing and/or stretching your knitting. It can take your finished piece from eh . . . to Wow! There are many factors that can affect whether or not to block, and what type of blocking method to use. The two methods I rely on are wet blocking and steam blocking.

Wet Blocking

Wet blocking is the method I personally use most frequently and it is safe on any fiber. Depending on the fiber, you will want to use either cold or warm water. Be sure to check your yarn label to see what it recommends. To wet block a glove or mitten, submerge it in water with a bit of wool wash. It's a good idea to use wool wash even on nonwool fibers because it is less harsh than detergent. Let the glove soak for a few minutes; don't leave it to soak for long. Rinse it out thoroughly. Some yarns will bleed color. Be sure to continue rinsing until the water runs clear. Gently fold the glove and press out excess water; don't wring your glove! Then roll it in a towel, soaking up as much moisture as you can. Lay your glove on a blocking mat or other surface that won't incur water damage. Carefully pat and lightly stretch the glove into shape, smoothing out any unevenness in the stitches. For colorwork gloves, blocking is especially important in evening out stitches. You may have to be a little more forceful when blocking these. Once your glove is in shape and smooth, let it dry. That's it!

Steam Blocking

There are special garment steamers available for steam blocking, but it's often hard to control temperature on these. An iron is nice because you can control the amount of steam and the temperature. It's typically not a good idea to go too steam-crazy on knitting, as it can give the knitted fabric a "wilted" effect and make it limp and lifeless. Again, be sure to check your yarn label to see what it recommends. But honestly, even for a yarn that does not recommend ironing, a light steaming is probably not going to harm it.

To steam block, lay out your glove. With the iron set on a low to medium setting, hold it at least 2 inches above the glove. Pass the iron slowly back and forth over the top of the piece. You will see the stitches react to the steam, sort of settling into place. After steaming, let the piece dry.

I will sometimes try steam blocking before wet blocking as it is not as time consuming and doesn't take as long to dry.

There are some projects in this book that do not mention blocking in the finishing instructions. This is because with the combination of stitch patterns and yarn used, I personally did not find it necessary to do so. This may not be true for you! If your glove turns out a little uneven here and there, even if the instructions don't specify to block, by all means do!